Understanding and Helping
the Retarded Reader

Understanding and Helping

THE ABLE RETARDED READER
THE EMOTIONALLY DISTURBED
THE BILINGUAL CHILD
THE MENTALLY RETARDED

the Retarded Reader

EDITED BY

RUTH STRANG

PROFESSOR OF EDUCATION AND
DIRECTOR OF THE READING DEVELOPMENT CENTER
THE UNIVERSITY OF ARIZONA

THE UNIVERSITY OF ARIZONA PRESS
TUCSON

THE UNIVERSITY OF ARIZONA PRESS

First printing 1965
Second printing 1965
Third printing 1965
Fourth printing 1967

Library of Congress Catalog
Card No. 64-17275

Manufactured in the United States of America

Preface

In our schools today we find many pupils who are reading a year or more below their grade placement. The majority of them might have been spared the experience of failure in reading had they been given effective instruction from the beginning; they have the potential mental ability to read at, or even above, the level appropriate to their age or grade. These are the able retarded readers. A smaller percentage are mentally retarded pupils who, with special instruction, can learn to read up to their mental capacity. In other cases, emotional difficulties are blocking progress in reading. In the schools of our Southwest, we have many pupils from Indian- and Spanish-speaking homes who are retarded in reading because English to them is a second language.

How can we identify, diagnose, and understand these children and young people, and how may we help them realize their potential reading ability? These are the themes of this book.

Understanding and Helping the Retarded Reader is the proceedings of a unique statewide Arizona Conference on reading problems. It was held in the spring of 1962 and was sponsored jointly by the Reading Development Center of the College of Education of Arizona, and the Arizona Intermediate Reading Council of the International Reading Association. The program chairmen were Dorothy Talbert, intermediate supervisor, Tucson District #1 and Ruth Strang, University of Arizona.

This book is divided into four parts, each of which deals with the reading development and reading difficulties of one group: I, able retarded readers; II, pupils with emotional problems; III, pupils from non-English-speaking homes; and IV, mentally retarded pupils. Each of these four parts is subdivided into three sections: (1) identification and diagnosis, (2) understanding of individuals who have this type of reading problem, and (3) procedures for helping them to improve their reading. In the third section, excerpts from demonstrations by experienced teachers and specialists who have worked with each of these kinds of reading problems are included. In the actual demonstration there is opportunity to observe how mentally retarded children, able retarded readers, emotionally disturbed children, and children from non-English-speaking homes responded to the various methods and materials. In print we can only present statements of each teacher's purposes and objectives, glimpses of the actual interaction, and points that were brought out in the discussions which followed each demonstration.

Part I, concerned with retarded readers who possess potential ability to read better, has three contributors. Helen C. Wright, director, Remedial Education Center, Tucson, describes methods and techniques of determining the nature of the individual's reading problem and of obtaining clues about its causation. Dr. Helen Robinson, William S. Gray Research Professor in Reading at the University of Chicago, makes available to classroom teachers the deep scientific understanding of able retarded readers which she has obtained from first-hand experience in the University of Chicago Reading Clinic, from her many years of giving university courses in the teaching of reading, and from her intensive reading and research in the field. No one else has her combination of accomplishments. The third contribution, by Rosemary Yoakum, remedial reading teacher, Tucson District #1, comprises excerpts from her demonstration lesson with a group of able retarded readers.

Part II deals with the reading problems of emotionally disturbed children. Peter Gallagher, school psychologist, Amphitheatre Public Schools, Tucson, describes emotional difficulties that are associated with reading, and offers some diagnostic procedures which he has found useful. Boris Zemsky, M.D., psychiatrist, Tucson Child Guidance Clinic, looks at the problem from the standpoint of special services that cooperate with classroom teachers, reading teachers, and school counselors. Ralph D. Rabinovitch, M.D., director of Hawthorn Center, Michigan, discusses the newer research and technical knowledge that are important to both teachers and clinicians. He also sheds light on the troublesome area of neurologically-determined reading difficulties. Reading instruction with emotionally disturbed children is illustrated by excerpts from a demonstration by Lora Anderson, remedial reading teacher, Tucson District #1.

Part III deals with the special problems of children from non-English-speaking homes. This topic is introduced by Mamie Sizemore who, as classroom specialist, Arizona Department of Education, Phoenix, has acquired a thorough understanding of the problems of children to whom English is a second language. She describes methods by which teachers have successfully helped these children learn to speak and read what, to them, is a foreign language. Dr. Miles Zintz, professor of elementary education, The University of New Mexico, who has carried forward Lloyd S. Tireman's pioneer work in teaching the language arts to Spanish-speaking children, describes recent developments in this field. Part III concludes with excerpts from a demonstration of teaching English to bilingual children by Jane Moore, Davis School, Tucson District #1.

Part IV, concerned with the mentally retarded pupil, is introduced by Mary Barreca, head teacher, Howenstein School, Tucson, who is especially competent in understanding mentally retarded children. She emphasizes the importance of evoking their best efforts without increasing their feelings of inferiority. Dr. Norris G. Haring, professor of education and educational director, Children's Rehabilitation Unit, University of Kansas Medical Center, from his varied experience in public schools, special services, university teaching, research projects, and medical clinics contributes practical suggestions, supported by sound theory, for gaining understanding of the reading problems of these children. Part II concludes with excerpts from a demonstration lesson with a group of mentally retarded children conducted by Frank Gunter, director of Special Education, Amphitheatre Public Schools, Tucson.

This book aims to give reading teachers and specialists:

1. A clearer recognition of the individual differences in reading performance among the pupils in their classes.
2. Skill in identifying and diagnosing potentialities and handicaps.
3. Deeper understanding of the multiple causation of reading problems.
4. Acquaintance with ways of helping pupils to overcome their reading handicaps.

To all the participants, the editor is greatly indebted for their unique contributions. Acknowledgment is also made to Dr. Amelia Melnik who was responsible for the demonstration program and the bibliography, and to others who helped plan and carry out the conference program and who served as resource persons and discussion leaders. Among these are Laura Ganoung, Thad Jennings, Edith Lyons, Iris Mulvaney, Winifred Rinker, Minnie Roseberry, Mamie Sizemore, Margaret Thornton, and James Trainer.

Ruth Strang

Contents

Introduction

The retarded reader is usually defined as one who has had normal opportunities for schooling and the capacity to read better, but whose reading performance in a number of reading skills is one or more years below his age or grade level if he is in the primary grades, and two years or more if he is older.

Among the retarded readers we find children from non-English-speaking homes; children from homes which gave them little or no incentive to learn; and children who have been deprived of essential preschool prereading experiences such as being read to, having interesting things to see and do and talk about, and associating with people who will listen to them and answer their questions. We also find children who are retarded because they got off to a poor start in school: they were absent a great deal; were handicapped by illness or uncorrected physical defects; were antagonized by the teacher; were given formal instruction in reading before they were mentally, physically, or socially ready for it. In other cases the psychological energy that should have been devoted to learning to read was used up in various kinds of emotional conflicts. There is also an undetermined number of children whose progress in reading has been impeded by brain injury or neurological disorganization or disturbance.

Among the retarded readers we also find children who have mistakenly come to conceive of themselves as non-readers; this false concept has destroyed all their hopes of ever learning to read. There are others who are using failure in reading to punish a parent or teacher who has aroused their hostility. Still others are above average in some reading skills though very poor in others. And some are merely reluctant readers; they can read but they don't.

These and many other individual patterns of retardation may be described under four main headings: able retarded readers, who have potential ability to read better, mentally retarded children, emotionally disturbed pupils, and bilingual children. The four chapters of this book will be concerned with the identification, understanding, and treatment of these four major categories. Recognizing the emotionally disturbed child, distinguishing between the mentally retarded child and the child who for any number of reasons is retarded in reading only, and understanding the linguistic and cultural difficulties of the child whose parents speak only a foreign language – these are the first steps toward better reading instruction.

Reading teachers and specialists need also a deeper understanding of the reading patterns and difficulties that are associated with each of our four categories. And, finally, there is no substitute for observing experienced reading teachers in action with various types of pupils and noting how able retarded readers, mentally retarded pupils, emotionally disturbed children, and bilingual children respond to various methods and materials.

Levels of Knowledge and Skill

Work with retarded readers is carried on by means of various techniques and materials of instruction, and on different levels of specialized knowledge. The most fundamental level is that represented by the work of the classroom teacher.

In his class he will find pupils like Donald, Mary, José, and Joanne. They are all the same age, and their reading scores are all two to three years below their age and grade placement. However, their reading problems are very different and require different treatment.

Donald is above average in mental ability and could be expected to read much better than he does. Mary tries to please the teacher and her parents, but it is hard for her to remember the words or to make sense of the sentences that she is expected to read. Her mental development may have been retarded, or her reading ability impaired by brain injury or some neurological deficit. José's family speaks nothing but Spanish; English is a second language to him. Reading does not make sense to him because he has no background in oral English. Joanne's mind is always busy with fantasies. She cannot concentrate on reading.

The teacher's chief means of gaining understanding are day-by-day observation; informal testing; conversations or conferences with pupils, parents, and colleagues; psychological examinations; medical reports on vision, hearing, and other physical conditions. From these sources the teacher gains information about the pupil's reading: how he reads, what he reads, why he reads, when he reads, the progress he is making, the difficulties he is having, and some clues about the conditions that are causing his difficulties.

The teacher's study of the pupil is not "an extra"; it is an intrinsic part of the teaching process. It goes on continuously during the school year. Its main purpose is to help each pupil develop his potential reading ability. Consequently there should be a balance between the time the teacher spends in gaining information and the time he spends in helping the retarded reader to reinforce his strengths and overcome his weaknesses and deficiencies.

The second level is that which concerns the reading teacher and consultant, or the counselor who has had some special preparation for teaching reading. He will supplement his observation of individuals and groups with longer and more diagnostic interviews and with reading tests, individual intelligence tests, listening comprehension tests, and other special methods that will be described later. Some of these can be used with groups; others must be administered individually.

Instead of going through a routine diagnostic procedure in the first session with an individual or group, the reading teacher who is aware of the pupil's needs and the help he expects will begin with the reading situation as the pupil sees it and as he wants to present it. In the process of helping the pupil to improve his reading, the teacher will learn more about the pupil's attitude toward reading and toward himself; he will determine the kind of material the pupil can read independently. The child who has suffered frustration and failure should be spared a repetition of these experiences. He needs success in order to rebuild his self-esteem, confidence, and security. From time to time as the need for more diagnostic information becomes evident, the reading teacher will use other appropriate tests and techniques.

The third or clinical level involves many of the same techniques: observation, interview, tests, and projective techniques. However, in interpreting the information gained from these sources, the clinician brings to bear a deeper psychological knowledge and more penetrating insights. He is also more aware of the therapeutic effect of his treatment and of the unconscious motivations of the client.

Diagnostic Procedures

Certain general diagnostic procedures are useful in identifying and understanding the different types of cases.

1. If the school gives all pupils a *standardized reading test,* the teacher can get information from this source. He finds that these retarded pupils fall two or three years below the average score made by a large number of pupils of the same age and grade. However, reading scores may be misleading, especially on the lower age levels. Teachers find that some pupils who obtain second-grade scores are unable

to read a second-grade book. The sub-scores on these tests, though of limited reliability, tell a little more about the pupil's proficiency in the varied aspects of reading that the tests measure. Analysis of the pupil's responses on standardized reading tests like the Sequential Tests of Educational Progress (STEP) reveals more about his specific difficulties.

2. *Informal silent reading tests* in each subject yield valuable information: how the pupil organizes and relates the ideas he has gained from reading; whether he comprehends the main ideas and the supporting details; whether he can make inferences and generalizations, appreciate the author's style, intent and purpose, and identify with or understand the characters.

3. *Oral reading tests* reveal specific word recognition difficulties; they show word-by-word reading, poor phrasing and expression; sometimes they indicate the pupil's attitudes toward himself and his reading. By occasionally listening to the pupil read aloud, by asking him questions on the material read, by having him report on or participate in discussions of the content, the teacher learns still more about the quality of the pupil's performance and the difficulties he is facing.

All of this information is valuable; it enables the teacher to help a pupil, as one youngster said, "to learn what I need to know, not what everybody else needs to know." However, none of this information about pupils' reading answers the question, "*Why* are pupils like Donald, Mary, José, and Joanne reading two to three years below their chronological age?" Is it because they are lacking in mental ability?

4. We turn hopefully to our *intelligence test* scores, IQs, or stanines. But most of the group intelligence tests require so much reading ability that they do not give the answers about seriously retarded readers. The poor reader is penalized; he does not demonstrate his actual mental ability. Tests that yield both a verbal and a quantitative score are a

little more useful; the quantitative score is less affected by poor reading than the verbal score. If we can obtain the detailed results of a Wechsler individual intelligence test, we have a little more indication of the pupil's potential reading ability. If the quantitative IQ is higher than the verbal, and if there is evidence that the pupil has been deprived of home and school opportunities to develop verbal ability, we can be hopeful about his chances for improvement in reading.

5. If his *comprehension when listening* is much better than his comprehension when reading similar material, the prognosis for improvement is still better.

6. Last, but certainly not least, is the *day-by-day observation* of the children's attitudes, habits, and performance in the classroom; *interviews with their parents;* and *home visits.*

Let us go back to the four children mentioned earlier. Donald's intelligence test scores and listening comprehension were above average. Day-by-day observation in the classroom showed a good memory, quickness to see relations and solve practical problems, word knowledge and effective use of words – all evidence of functioning intelligence. We might reasonably conclude that Donald has the mental ability to read better.

In Mary's case we should guard against concluding that she lacks the mental ability to read better, just because her intelligence test scores have been low. To reach such a conclusion we should need a much more thorough study, including a medical and developmental history, and a year's observation in a school situation. Some children exceed their measured mental age in reading achievement, while others do not read as well as might be expected even with the best instruction.

The best way to judge whether a child has the ability to read better is to give him our best instruction and see whether he learns.

José's difficulty in reading seems more obvious. Study of his home background, observation of his behavior in the classroom and on the playground, and analysis of the ways in which English and his native language differ with respect to pronunciation and sentence patterns would give us specific information about his use of English and his difficulties in pronunciation and sentence structure. From the same sources we should obtain evidence of his mental alertness and emotional adjustment. We also need to know about his emotional attachment to his native language, the attitude of his family and friends toward his learning English, and various other subtle influences that may be peculiar to his culture, if we are to help him make optimum progress in reading.

Joanne's emotional problems would be best revealed by daily observation, interviews, and home visits or parent conferences. If expert psychological or psychiatric assistance is available, interview, play therapy, and projective methods might yield more understanding of the emotional conflicts that may be interfering with her reading. Through introspective reports, made in a secure relationship or in response to a provocative picture or story, children often give clues to their deeper feelings. In these cases we would note such characteristics as shyness, withdrawal, anxiety, timidity, fear, apathy, and aggressive behavior stemming from frustration. We should also be alert to discover evidences of parental perfectionism, inconsistency, or favoritism.

It is obvious that reading retardation seldom has a single cause. This fact is evident in the case of many children like Donald who have the mental ability to read better but do not attain their reading potential for various reasons: immaturity, poor instruction, failure to recognize and correct early reading difficulty, poor health, auditory or visual defects, disturbed family relations, and other conditions. However, one factor may be dominant or central to the reading problem in an individual case.

Essentials of Treatment

Certain essentials apply to the treatment of many kinds of cases. What we might call "the learning triangle" involves the pupil or client, the teacher or clinician, and the method used. These three interact in complex ways. The importance of pupil-teacher, client-counselor, and client-therapist relationships is receiving increasing recognition. With many kinds of cases it has been found that the teacher, counselor, or therapist is more likely to be successful if he shows a genuine concern for the individual and has the ability to communicate his acceptance and respect for him.

Getting to know you,
Getting to know all about you.
Getting to like you,
Getting to hope you like me.

These lines from the musical, *The King and I*, express two other related conditions for learning: understanding and mutual affection. The atmosphere that prevails in a group or in an individual relationship has an appreciable effect on the progress made by the retarded reader. He cannot learn as long as he is constantly threatened by failure, negative criticism, and the ridicule of his classmates, as long as he is inhibited by fear. In an atmosphere of optimism he is encouraged to do his best. As one youngster said, "Miss S. believed I could improve my reading, and I didn't want to let her down."

It is also essential to try to understand the whole personality of the retarded reader. Reading is an expression of individuality; reading difficulty often is a symptom of a personality disturbance. Thus whatever is done to build up the pupil's personality – to help him become more self-confident, hopeful, and successful in other ways – is likely to contribute to his reading improvement.

The most obvious essential of treatment is to give effective instruction in those developmental reading skills which the individual needs and in which he is deficient. These may be poor auditory or visual perception, faulty conceptualization, or lack of basic sight vocabulary and word recognition skills. Quite often, the retarded reader is unable to apply the simple sound-symbol associations he has learned to the complex task of reading. For "reading is reasoning." It requires a background of experience, ability to see relationships, and shrewdness to anticipate and check meaning in the context. The higher levels of reading require ability to sense the author's mood and purpose, to read between the lines and beyond the lines. Reading, in its broadest sense, implies an emotional response and a desire to apply the ideas thus gained to life problems. The teacher or clinician who detects a weakness in any of these aspects of reading will try to provide the instruction necessary to correct it.

Reading Materials

Suitable reading materials are absolutely essential in the treatment of the retarded reader. If the books are too difficult, they intensify his already keen sense of failure and inadequacy. If they are too easy, or if they are dull or remote from his areas of interest, they offer him no incentive or reward for putting forth the effort that efficient reading demands. The retarded reader who has to plod through an unsuitable book confirms his previous opinion that "reading is for the birds." Recommending a book to a retarded reader is a serious matter.

In a panel discussion, a group of bright elementary and junior high school pupils made some enlightening comments on books they had read. Their discussion may suggest something about the kinds of reading material that appeal to children and young adolescents.

Mystery, suspense, and exciting adventure appealed to them. These are generally the "big three" in boys' reading interests. However, they are also aware of other qualities. One pupil said he liked characters whose feelings were so life-like that the reader knew just how they felt. Another pupil said, "The author does not try to make a hero out of the chief character but just showed – to put it bluntly – that he was no good." They were also interested in certain kinds of non-fiction such as descriptions of the life of lizards and armadillos.

Finally, they gave their advice to authors. Following are some of their specific criticisms:

"The author gets way off the track. His book is supposed

to be about rabbits. When he does talk about rabbits, it's about jack rabbits. He should stick to the subject."

"Some authors seem to think the children who read their books are not very smart; they talk down to them."

"I don't like books when I can guess the ending after reading the first ten pages."

"Some authors use too many *ands* and *buts*, and do the opposite of what our English teacher tells us about not repeating the same words too often."

"Some books are boring in the beginning; the author should put more excitement and adventure into the first pages."

"Some authors should carry through better and tell more about the event they introduce in the beginning."

Concluding Statement

Retarded readers such as we have described are especially susceptible to conditions that block, distract, or frustrate them. The first step is to appraise the pupil's positive qualities and diagnose his reading difficulties. The understanding thus gained should be put to immediate use. There should be no gap between obtaining information and using it to help the pupil make progress toward achieving his potential reading ability. As Confucius once said, "There is no greater happiness than to see a child go confidently forward on the right path after we have made clear the way."

The following chapters give much more detail about identifying, understanding, and finding ways to help able retarded readers, those who are mentally retarded, those who are emotionally disturbed, and those who come from non-English-speaking homes.

Chapter One:

In our schools today we find a large number of students, how many has not been exactly determined, whose achievement does not match their intellectual capacity. They are not mentally retarded; they have not suffered brain damage or disorganization severe enough to cause permanent impairment of their intellectual functioning; their reading disabilities are not due to visual, auditory, or other physical defects. If they show any emotional disturbance, it is likely to be the consequence rather than the cause of their reading retardation. They are more likely to be deeply discouraged and frustrated than reluctant or resistant.

The Able Retarded Reader

The able retarded reader has the potential ability to achieve at or above his grade and age level. But he has failed to meet the school requirements in reading, and often in spelling and the other language arts as well. He may be unchallenged, unmotivated; or he may be inhibited by unfavorable conditions in the school or at home.

The retarded reader who is capable of making much better progress presents an urgent problem to our schools today. He needs to be identified, understood, and helped to attain his reading potentialities.

HELEN C. WRIGHT

Identification and Diagnosis of the Able Retarded Reader

Any attempt to identify the able child who is retarded in reading rests upon two major tests. In the first place we must determine his average or above-average caliber by means of a test of his intellectual functioning in which reading is not involved. We frequently use the Wechsler Intelligence Scale for Children and the Wechsler Adult Intelligence Scale (for 16 years and above) for this purpose. Besides giving the present level of intellectual functioning and indicating potential capacity, these tests permit differentiation of cognitive abilities and occasionally give some hints about personality type.

The second basic identification instrument is a diagnostic test of reading which should serve to separate vocabulary and comprehension skills from rate. There are many tests which perform this function, including the New Gray Oral Reading test (4)*, the Gates Diagnostic (3), the Gates Reading Survey (3), the Durrell-Sullivan Reading Tests (2), the Diagnostic Reading Tests (1) and, at the secondary and college level, STEP (8) or other reading tests.

*Numbers in parentheses refer to references at the end of the section.

We must seek the tests which will tell us most clearly the significant facts that we need and will do so in the most efficient way. At the Remedial Education Center we try to avoid, wherever possible, tests and materials currently employed by the various school systems. This means we must be alert to find the best, and to assess the new and frequently to devise our own. But certain standardized tests are essential.

Besides an individual intelligence test and a diagnostic silent reading test, the student is given a standardized oral reading test. The client's errors are noted, classified, and carefully analyzed. An informal inventory is also given from which his basal, independent, instructional, and frustration levels are determined. A standardized spelling test such as the Wide Range Achievement Test (10), the Stanford Achievement Test (9), or the Morrison-McCall Spelling Scale (7) is added to the test battery. Again errors are analyzed. The client's knowledge and use of sound-letter associations and word structure are tested with a word analysis inventory.

The client's directional orientation is observed throughout by means of tests which are adaptations of the Harris Tests of Lateral Dominance. The examiner notes whether the student knows right from left and which hand, foot, and eye he uses in various activities. Preferred eye in both monocular and binocular vision is checked.

Does the child reverse words totally or partially in reading? Does he transpose words in a phrase? Does he transpose letters in spelling? Does he confuse *d* and *b* and *p*, or *n* and *u* or *h* and *y*? Does he mind his *p's* and *q's*? Does he write digits as seen in a mirror? Harris' Simultaneous Writing Test (5) is interesting here, although we have not made it a regular part of our battery. And do these symptoms persist beyond the lack of sophistication characteristic of the primary grades?

Does handwriting show other confusions of left to right progression? Does he cross *t's* from right to left? Does he make *o's* clockwise instead of counter-clockwise? Does handwriting indicate dysgraphia? Is there an irregularity, a lack of motor coordination? Does he persist in an odd use of his pencil or an odd hand position? Does he demand an unusual position of the paper?

Of interest also is figure-ground orientation, as well as closure in assessing his skill in visual perception, in distinguishing readily the figure – pattern, word, or phrase – from the background. Can he employ closure, can he read a word or phrase cut off at the top; can he detect appropriate clues so that key letters or part of the word or phrase pattern will indicate to him the whole, ignoring the missing or unobserved parts?

Is his vision clear, binocular, free from strain at close range? Is his hearing distinct; is it mature in regard to speech sounds? Does he persist in infantile substitutions and confusions, or is his pronunciation relatively adult?

Basic to any diagnosis or plan is a full case history. We want to know the student's developmental history. Was he a full-term baby, did he have a normal birth, was he breast fed? At what age did he walk and talk? When and how was toilet training accomplished?

What has been his health history? Did he have colic, prolonged crying spells? Has he had a good appetite and throughout what ages? What illnesses has he experienced and at what ages? What major accidents has he had? What clues as to his reading difficulties are suggested by the family history, relation with siblings and parents, attitudes of persons toward the child, other aspects of the home environment, education and occupation of parents, and activities of the family group?

His school history may begin with his attitude and adjustment in nursery school or first grade. What has been his attitude toward school? Does he enjoy school? Is he reluctant? Has his attendance been regular? Has he been in one school or in many?

What information does the school report give about him? How well does he adjust to the teacher, the classroom, on the playground? How well is he liked by his peers? How responsible is he?

What is the history of his reading problem? When was it first observed? What has been done about it? Has he had other special attention, tutoring? By whom?

How does the parent feel about his reading problem –

anxious, angry, punitive, calm, or overly solicitous? Does the mother say, "He takes after his father's family. None of them could read very well either." Or, "He was crowded out by his younger sister and now she reads better than he does. He's smaller than his younger brother. There isn't anything in which he excels."

Not least, and not least important, is the child's own attitude and his self-report or evaluation of his situation, for we must begin with him – not only where he is, but where he considers himself to be. As one fourth grader put it, "I simply hate reading, that's all." Other older students often express quite clearly statements of their problem. "When I try to read it out loud the words get all mixed up and out of place." Or, conversely, "Unless I read out loud, it doesn't make any sense." Or, "I can't ever finish in time."

It is essential to recognize our own diagnostic limitations and to know when to call upon the other allied disciplines to fill in or to correct the picture. We constantly need the advice of the pediatrician, the audiologist, the opthalmologist, the counselor, school administrator, psychologist, psychiatrist, the professor, the social case worker, and the library science expert.

What does it all add up to? Hopefully, to at least a starting point, a tentative diagnosis, and a plan based upon the findings of the tests, the confirmation of the case history, and the advice of specialists from other disciplines.

But this is just the beginning. Diagnosis is a continuous, ongoing, never-ending process during remediation, consisting of the weekly review and reassessment of every student, as well as his periodic consideration at weekly staff conferences.

References

1. *Diagnostic Reading Tests*. Committee on Diagnostic Reading Tests, Inc. Mountain Home, North Carolina: Frances Triggs.
2. *Durrell-Sullivan Reading Tests*. Yonkers-on-Hudson, N.Y.: World Book Company.

3. *Gates Reading Survey Test* and *Gates Diagnostic Reading Test.* New York: Bureau of Publications, Teachers College, Columbia University.

4. *New Gray Oral Reading Test.* Indianapolis 6, Ind.: The Bobbs-Merrill Company, Inc.

5. *Harris Tests of Lateral Dominance, Simultaneous Writing* (a subtest). New York 18, N.Y.: The Psychological Corporation.

6. Harris, Albert J., "Perceptual Difficulties in Reading" in *Changing Concepts of Reading Instruction*, pp. 282-290, edited by J. Allen Figurel. International Reading Association Conference Proceedings, Vol. 6. New York 36, N.Y.: Scholastic Magazines, 1961.

7. *Morrison-McCall Spelling Scale.* Yonkers-on-Hudson, N.Y.: World Book Company.

8. *Sequential Tests of Educational Progress.* Princeton, N.J.: Cooperative Test Division.

9. *Stanford Achievement Test*, 1953 revision. Tarrytown, N.Y.: Harcourt, Brace & World, Inc.

10. *Wide-range Achievement Test*, 1946 edition. New York: Psychological Corporation.

HELEN M. ROBINSON

Understanding the Able Retarded Reader

An urgent problem in schools today is the retarded reader who is capable of making much better progress than he is making. Most retarded readers have I.Q.'s in the range from 75 or 80 to 165 or 170. For the most part, these children and young people score within the normal range on intelligence tests, especially tests that do not require reading. Obviously these pupils will be greatly handicapped on many tests that require reading, regardless of the other abilities that such tests are supposed to measure.

One of the commonest misconceptions is that a large proportion of retarded readers are really slow learners. In your classroom, where approximately half of the children will score at or below the norm on a standardized reading test, you have a real challenge to distinguish the retarded readers from the slow learners. The latter, if they have proper instruction, are making as much progress in reading as can be expected.

What are some of the characteristics that retarded readers are likely to display? First, the retarded reader usually learns more from listening than from reading. In an accepting atmosphere, he also talks much better than he reads. Severely retarded readers develop an ability to listen and to remember what they hear – information, directions, and the like – because they are not able to take notes or to read directions. They profit from discussions in which the class participates, and they learn from all kinds of oral reports or from materials that are read to them by classmates and teachers. When such pupils are given an oral examination on content, the results often surprise their teachers who are accustomed to meager and inadequate answers on tests which require reading and writing rather than listening and speaking. Retarded readers who are kept in classes with their age mates often score higher on tests of arithmetic computation than on other types of tests because this is the area least affected by reading handicaps.

Many retarded readers do not complete assignments and therefore are dubbed by an occasional teacher and many parents as "lazy." Actually, these children are frustrated as a result of repeated failures; they are unable to read the usual assignment. The retarded reader may give you a dozen good reasons why he does not need to learn to read; these are his front-line defense against further frustration and failure. Basically he wants to learn because he has a strong desire to be like his age mates. Besides, he wishes to prove to himself and others that he is really not dumb.

A classroom teacher can learn a great deal about a retarded reader. To do this, however, he must allot time from his busy schedule, perhaps five or ten minutes per day, to concentrate on the study of one pupil at a time. As information is obtained, it should be jotted down while it is fresh in mind. Later the teacher can put together all this information; it often gives new insight into the pupil's problems.

The major purpose of diagnosis is to determine, first, where to begin in overcoming the difficulties; second, what skills and abilities need to be taught; and third, which method is most likely to help the child learn rapidly. The classroom teacher can often make good use of an informal reading test constructed from paragraphs or short stories in a set of basal readers that is not being used in the classroom for instruction. It is always wise to begin with an easy sample, perhaps one or two grades below the level at which you think the pupil is actually reading. Then gradually increase the difficulty until the material becomes too hard. One sample or page may be read orally and another silently. This enables you to compare oral and silent reading, and to explore difficulties in each area. Questions asked about the material read should test comprehension of the content and should cover a wide range of skills or abilities. Unless this is done, you may not be covering the areas you need most to assess. For further explanation of this procedure and for samples, you may wish to look at a book by Nila B. Smith and others (3) and Emmett Betts' *Handbook for Corrective Reading* (1).

The classroom teacher also should check with the school nurse; if data are not already available on vision and hearing, they should be obtained. Any physical difficulties that are found should be corrected promptly; otherwise the teacher may have to compensate for them in her work with the pupil.

Relatively simple diagnosis should accompany every remedial lesson; it furnishes a basis for selecting the procedures to be used as the student makes progress. In a sense, diagnosis is a continuous process, concurrent with remedial instruction.

If you are not able to secure the information you need or if you need help in this task, ask your principal, the school psychologist, the remedial reading teacher, or anyone else who may be available to give you added insight and assistance. It is true that some retarded readers need more expert diagnosis than the classroom teacher can give. Schools that have specially prepared remedial teachers are indeed fortunate. However, most schools have access to a reading clinic, either privately operated or, preferably, conducted by a major university. A clinic is prepared to do a more thorough diagnosis than is done in most schools.

In the short space available, some of the principles for helping retarded readers improve their reading will be discussed. The first principle is to utilize all available information to establish the proper climate and to develop an interpersonal relationship which is conducive to reading success. To do this you must accept the retarded reader as a person who has certain problems, whether they be academic, personal, or both. Most of these pupils feel that previous teachers have disliked them. By convincing them that you like them, you can free energies which they can apply to learning (2).*

It is also necessary to respect the integrity of each pupil. Too often he has been told that he is "no good" or "dumb" or a "trouble maker." Perhaps his teachers have not made these remarks to him directly, but he has interpreted their statements to mean this, probably because of the manner in which they were made. A complete reversal of this attitude is essential; no child puts forth effort without some hope of success.

Most retarded readers fear any activity associated with reading because of their previous frustrations. An accepting teacher permits each pupil to express his fears or dislikes. She even permits him to express resentment toward teachers, his family, his peers, or anyone else who is associated in his mind with failure and frustration. A teacher who wishes to understand the pupil does not criticize him for expressing such hostility, nor does she contradict him in order to support her colleagues or others. Her purpose is to understand how he feels and thinks. One word of caution, however; the teacher does not probe for these expressions; she accepts them as they come to her either directly or indirectly.

One very common characteristic of retarded readers is fear of making a mistake. Consequently many of them prefer to do only the tasks which they think they can do successfully. In their previous experiences there has obviously been a great premium on accuracy; they have interpreted unfavorable comments on their errors as personal disapproval. Hence a pupil may be afraid to try to read if he is sure that many of his responses will be wrong. An accepting teacher can elicit

*Excerpts are quoted with the permission of the managing editor of *Education* from Helen M. Robinson's article, "Fundamental Principles for Helping Retarded Readers," *Education*, 72 (May, 1952), 596–599.

greater effort from a pupil by accepting his errors. As he becomes aware that his mistakes are important clues in helping the teacher determine the particular areas in which he has not been taught satisfactorily, the pupil becomes increasingly relaxed.

The second principle for helping retarded readers is to determine which methods and materials are best suited to each individual (2, p. 597). When the pupil is free to apply his energies to learning, it is essential that everything be done to hasten his improvement. To insure balanced development in all aspects of reading, long-term goals should be set. Each one can then be divided into a series of short-term goals which become the basis for planning daily lessons. After rapport is established between teacher and pupil, it is helpful in most cases to explain what is to be accomplished; the pupil's understanding of what you are trying to do is basic to full cooperation. As a pupil shares the initial goals with the teacher, he may begin to take active responsibility in setting his own goals. Pupils are willing to exert greater effort if their goals are self-imposed. Many examples could be cited in which a pupil has put forth vigorous effort to learn to recognize certain words, to finish reading a given book, or to interpret a particular passage because he has set for himself a time limit for completing this phase of his reading. It is important that early goals be structured so that they can be readily accomplished with due effort. As progress is made, the goals may become increasingly exacting. This is done without applying pressure, except as the pupil himself supplies it.

An analysis of any short-term goal enables the remedial teacher to select one or more methods for attaining it. The case history and the diagnostic data should help the teacher choose the methods which appear to be most likely to succeed. It is then necessary to experiment with the chosen method and, if necessary, modify it until progress in reading is noted. The method helps to guide the teacher in choosing appropriate materials. In instances where several types of material appear to be equally satisfactory, the pupil should be permitted to select those he finds most interesting. However, the teacher must be cautious about accepting as authentic the pupil's verbalized interests; they are often dictated by his notions of what will be most acceptable to the teacher. In a relaxed atmosphere, however, real interests are revealed and pupil selection of materials may be greatly hastened.

Instruction should always begin at a level where the pupil can succeed (2, p. 598). This level is directly established by means of formal and informal tests, and is more accurately defined at each teaching period. It is not enough just to provide simple materials. The pupil may become very adept at reading simplified books and may read them indefinitely without moving forward to more complicated material. He must be challenged to progress gradually to more advanced levels and to master the reading skills appropriate to them. The teacher must enable the pupil to experience repeated successes and at the same time provide him with a constant challenge to move forward; this balance of forces is more easily described than achieved. It is probably one of the most important aspects of successful remedial instruction in reading.

At all times, retarded readers must be encouraged by praise when it is honestly earned. Praise should be neither lavish nor undeserved; insincere praise becomes meaningless. Retarded readers are adept at evaluating the sincerity of their teachers. However, tasks should be set in such a way that each instructional period includes an opportunity for the teacher to praise the pupil for the task accomplished as well as for the effort exerted. In addition, it is important that the pupil have tangible evidence of successful achievement. Keeping records of the number of words he has learned, making successive recordings of his oral reading, using charts or graphs to show his progress, or having the satisfying experience of completing a book – all these are concrete indications of specific accomplishment that encourage pupils far more than vague praise.

Most retarded readers dislike and fear tests because of unpleasant experiences with them. For this reason the teacher may profitably explain why tests are used, that she does not expect all the questions to be answered, and that the results will be useful in measuring the pupil's gains. If standardized tests are used, exact directions must be followed at all times. Some preliminary preparation tends to help the pupil become more relaxed, so that measurement will be more accurate. Furthermore, it is often quite reassuring to show a pupil the gains he has made. This latter procedure is not applicable to all pupils, but usually holds for older ones.

The pupil who has shared in setting his own goals and knows his scores on reading tests is capable of adding his opinion to those of his reading teacher, his classroom teacher, and his parents when the time comes to decide whether his remedial instruction is completed. When the pupil has an important role in making this decision and accepts the conclusion of remedial instruction as meaning that he has achieved his goal, he is unlikely to feel that discontinuance of special instruction means rejection by the teacher.

Successful remedial instruction in reading is achieved by setting goals, selecting appropriate methods for achieving each goal, and identifying the most useful materials for each purpose. Pupil participation in each stage of the learning process increases motivation for accomplishment.

References

1. Betts, Emmett. *Handbook for Corrective Reading*. American Education Series. Chicago: Wheeler Publishing Company, 1956.
2. Robinson, Helen M. "Fundamental Principles for Helping Retarded Readers," *Education*, 72 (May, 1952), 596-599.
3. Smith, Nila B. and others. *Graded Selections for Informal Reading Diagnosis*. New York: New York University Press, 1959.

DEMONSTRATED BY

ROSEMARY YOAKUM

Classroom Procedures with Able Retarded Readers

THE GROUP

Eight pupils in the seventh grade. The range in I.Q. on the Weschler Intelligence Scale for Children is from 95–124; the scores on standardized reading tests, from fifth through eighth grade. Their actual performance on the informal individual reading inventory showed their functioning independent level to be much lower than the test scores indicated. Each scored a little higher on a listening comprehension test than he did on a silent reading test or on the informal individual reading inventory. This group of retarded readers is "biologically intact," and so far as we know there are no neurological reasons why they cannot read better.

Their other teachers have described them as having poor work habits, not accepted by their peers, shy, unable to do the reading assignments and never completing them. Conditions in their home backgrounds such as illness, family disorganization, and frequent change of residence have contributed to their reading difficulties.

The pupils have commented as follows about their reading:

"I'd like to read faster."

"I'd also like to understand what I read better."

"I could read better if I wanted to."

"Nobody cared about my reading when I was young."

SPECIFIC OBJECTIVES

1. To learn to recognize the author's purpose in writing a paragraph.
2. To recognize the essential and subordinate ideas of a paragraph.
3. To become aware of the relation between the author's purpose and meaning and the structure that he creates to communicate his ideas to the reader.
4. To become acquainted with a variety of paragraph structure.
5. To discover skills essential to comprehension of the paragraph.
6. To reinforce their purpose for reading as an aid to comprehension.

ILLUSTRATIONS OF PROCEDURES

Teacher: In reading a paragraph, we want to understand what the author might want to tell us. I have here the paragraphs you picked out from magazines and newspapers and pasted the title or the headline on the back of each paragraph. What do you think a writer's purpose is when he writes a headline for his newspaper article?

Pupil: He tries to make it interesting, so you will read it.

T: Right. I'm sure he does that. Does he have any other purpose when he writes his heading or title? Let us read one of the paragraphs to find out. (Reads a paragraph about the body's defenses against disease.) What do you think the author of this paragraph wants to tell you, the listener?

P: About our body defenses against infection.
T: Yes. Any other ideas?
P: How your body protects against infection.
P: Explanation of some diseases.
T: (Discusses which of the three suggestions best describes the author's purpose.) Now look over the first paragraph on your list. Are there any words you don't know? In the first sentence, what does the word *banded* mean? (If the pupil could not give the meaning in his own words, the teacher made the task easier by giving him a choice of three possible meanings, one of which was right.) In the second paragraph, a *prairie schooner* is mentioned. What is that?
P: A covered wagon.
T: Read the paragraph and raise your hand when you've found the main idea.
P: The weasel is a bandit. (Other pupils agree.)
T: In the last two paragraphs, where was the main idea located?
P: In the last sentence.
T: What are some of the facts the author gives to prove that this weasel is a bandit?
P: It kills when it does not need to kill. It kills just for the fun of it.
T: Good.
P: It kills at night time.
P: It goes around the chicken house at night and kills chickens.
T: Why do you think the author tells about the chickens after he tells about the rabbits?
P: No difference.
T: Do you all agree it doesn't make any difference which he tells first? Can anyone give a reason for mentioning the killing of hens after he tells about the killing of rabbits?
P: To show he kills more than he eats.
T: Yes, any other reason?
P: He hates animals and they hate him . . .
T: In the second paragraph, is there any organization that

proves the author's main point better than any other? Where is the main idea?

P: In the last sentence.

T: Yes, the writer gives the details first and then the main idea. More often you find the main idea in the first or second sentence of the paragraph. Here is a paragraph that has been typed as separate sentences. See if you can put it together in the way the author did. (Pupils rearrange sentences into a paragraph, then check with the original paragraph.) Here are some patterns of paragraphs a high school group worked out and then gave each paragraph a name (1). Billy, will you read the names they gave each of these paragraphs?

P: (Reads names of types of paragraphs.)

T: Which of these patterns is a picture of the two paragraphs we've read thus far?

P: Main idea in a key sentence and then details.

T: And?

P: Details first and main idea in last sentence.

T: Right. (Examines other paragraphs with the pupils.)

QUESTIONS AND COMMENTS

In the demonstration, some characteristics of able retarded readers could be observed. They were shy, retiring, relatively unresponsive, and withdrawn. However, under ordinary classroom conditions, these characteristics are less pronounced. During the year these pupils have become less shy as they have made progress in reading. They do not feel embarrassed by going to a special reading class because there is no stigma attached to it. They have the feeling that it is a privilege to get into the special class.

What should be the relation between the special reading class and the other regular classes to which the pupil goes? The relationship should be close. Reading skills learned in the reading class should be used in the pupil's other classes. Books for the retarded readers in the regular classroom are recommended by the reading teacher. Teachers of every subject have responsibility for teaching pupils how to read their subject. The special class serves as a laboratory in which methods and materials can be developed and shared with other teachers. The need for a reading consultant in each school who would work with and through teachers as well as with retarded readers is evident.

What materials are used in the special class? Is a basal reader used? We do not use a single text. Each pupil is reading on a different level and has different reading problems. We try to select or prepare reading material especially selected for him.

How much word analysis do you teach? We try to help pupils become "on their own in reading" by teaching a combination of phonics, structural analysis, vocabulary study, and context clues.

How do you appraise progress? We note changes in scores on comparable forms of reading tests and on informal tests; but we also observe changes both in the personality of the individual pupil and also in his attitude toward himself and toward reading generally.

Reference

1. Strang, Ruth and Dorothy Bracken. *Making Better Readers.* Boston: D. C. Heath and Company, 1957, pp. 126-137.

Chapter Two:

There have been varying estimates of the extent to which emotional difficulties are associated with retardation in reading, all the way from 8 per cent of the cases referred to one public school reading clinic to 99 per cent of the cases referred to a psycho-linguistic clinic. Reports of research have indicated a higher incidence of neurological deficit or disturbance in reading disability cases than we previously thought. The incidence of emotional difficulty would normally increase with the severity of the reading problem.

However, attempts to describe a type of personality or a type of maladjustment characteristic of children with reading disabilities have failed. Studies comparing certain personality

Emotionally Disturbed Children

traits of poor readers with those of good readers have not shown any consistent group differences.

But clinical studies have revealed connections between the child's emotional pattern and his reading proficiency. Among children with serious reading problems one finds a few who are emotionally healthy; some who are very inhibited but otherwise apparently well adjusted; some who have various personality disorders; some whose behavior is definitely delinquent; and a few who are pre-psychotic or psychotic. In short, reading disability is found in combination with practically all degrees of emotional health.

PETER GALLAGHER

Identification of Emotional Difficulties in Reading

Teachers in recent years have tended to blame reading problems on emotional blocking. Unfortunately, the term "emotional block" is a very vague one. It is only the beginning of a description of what is wrong. Since there are different kinds of so-called emotional blocking, corrective procedures should differ according to the particular kind of blocking. Even when an emotional problem has been identified and seems to have a close relationship to the reading difficulty, one must remember that there are other children with similar emotional problems who read well.

Sometimes an emotional problem is combined with an eye defect or directional confusion, or absence from school at crucial periods of reading instruction, or – sometimes – dislike of an ineffectual teacher. Any of these conditions may center the problem on reading. And because successful reading requires application and sustained concentration, any problems which prevent a child from concentrating during reading lessons will also prevent him from learning to read.

Because reading is the first of the three R's to be systematically taught to children and the one with which parents and teachers are most deeply concerned, it quite naturally becomes the first educational issue around which the child tries to work out problems of reluctance to grow up or resistance to going to school or defiance of adult authority. Although the attempt to describe carefully and accurately the different kinds of emotional problems that may contribute to reading disabilities is just in its early stages, several different patterns can be distinguished.

1. *Conscious or unconscious refusal to learn.* The child may feel a real hostility to parents or teachers or both. Such hostility may cause the child to reject reading because it is identified with the adult or adults against whom his feelings are directed. This sometimes occurs when there is conflict between the cultural values of teacher and pupil. The child from a low socioeconomic background may not be willing to accept the goals which the teachers approve. Another cause might be displacement of hostility. The child, jealous of a brother or sister who is very good in reading, may transfer his hostility to the act of reading, which is the sibling's strong point.

2. *Resistance to pressure.* The overzealous parent who wants Johnny to be a quiz kid may arouse a resistance to pressure for intellectual attainment that may take the form of a disinterest in reading.

3. *A clinging to dependency.* The child who is over protected and babied may consciously or unconsciously prefer to remain infantile, thus getting attention through his helplessness.

4. *Extreme distractibility or restlessness.* A high degree of tension in the child may build up an uncontrollable need for relief in the form of physical activity. If the child cannot attend to his reading lessons, he will not learn.

This is not an exhaustive listing; other patterns will occur to you. Since reading disability is not a unique entity and since it is found in combination with practically all forms of child maladjustment, it is frequently difficult to point to a particular emotional variable as being the cause.

Diagnosing emotional difficulties in reading is largely a process of elimination. That is, by eliminating possible physical, neurological, and intellectual variables, an hypothesis of reading disability founded in emotional involvement is reached almost by default.

A psychological test battery which I have found useful includes the Weschler tests of intelligence, the Bender Visual Motor Gestalt Test, the Thematic Apperception Test (TAT), the Rorschach, figure drawings, and certain standard questions designed to elicit underlying feelings and attitudes. In addition to psychological tests, a comprehensive study would include a physical and a neurological examination.

A seventeen-year-old boy whom I recently tested illustrates a procedure for studying the relation of emotional problems to reading and general academic success. This boy was given the Weschler Intelligence Scale for Children (the WISC), the incomplete sentences, figure drawings, TAT stories, the Bender designs, the Rorschach, and also the Minnesota Multiphasic Personality Inventory. The Bender Gestalt Test is useful to the psychologist in giving clues as to organic dysfunctions and brain damage, but it is by no means a substitute for neurological examination.

In January, 1962, this boy scored at the sixth grade in both reading and arithmetic reasoning on the Stanford Achievement Test. On the WISC his full scale I.Q. was 103, though his potential ability may have been a little bit higher. His responses on the incomplete sentences suggested feelings of inferiority: "I failed today." "I can't do it. Other kids can do it." "I need people, but my greatest fear is people." "My greatest worry is getting a job and will people like me." Many of his other responses were in this general vein. From the sentence completion test alone, one can begin to infer severe personality problems.

The next test given was the figure drawings. These are useful to give clues as to the level of maturity of the individual. This boy's drawings were done on a very primitive level, in line with his general immaturity. The TAT stories suggested feelings of extreme hostility against his parents and a very poor image of himself. His Bender designs were very well reproduced, negating the hypothesis of organic involvement; however, they were rendered in a primitive, careless way. This boy's Rorschach was interesting in that it suggested an extreme of affectional need and a tendency to handle his problems by putting them at a distance. Although he had this need for love and warmth and closeness, he had apparently an intolerance for the very thing he needed. The MMPI more or less confirmed the impression obtained from the other tests. In the total picture it seemed quite obvious that emotional problems were interfering with this boy's academic and reading achievement.

The particular therapeutic approach to emotionally disturbed children is determined largely by the need that is being served by their reading disability. There are more or less transient stress situations, such as the birth of a sibling, at which time the child may express his anger at the frustration of his normal need for attention by developing a reading problem. The mother might be quite unaware that the attention lavished on the newborn child might be depriving other children of an adequate share of love. This problem is sometimes partly solved by advising the mother to try to give more of herself to the child, or by asking the teacher to give the child extra support and attention.

Other children should be referred to a remedial reading specialist who can meet their emotional needs with acceptance and love inherent in the relationship, as well as by skillful instruction in reading.

Children demonstrating personality disorder are perhaps the most difficult with whom to deal. They lack motivation and social responsiveness. Instead of emotional or intellectual disturbance, they show little or no anxiety or sense of distress. The child who manifests personality disorder seldom responds to direct remedial efforts. His lack of motivation, negativism, inadequacy, poor powers of concentration, and low persistence and drive are so ingrained as to become a way of life. Treatment in these cases typically involves working with the parents so that, hopefully, a more rational environment will be provided for the child.

Reading disability may be a symptom which may eventually lead to a veritable Pandora's Box of individual problems, some of which are handled with relative ease; others still defy our most enlightened methods. An integration of all social services is needed for a speedier resolution of these problems. This involves the heretofore unrealized goal of full cooperation and mutual respect among the disciplines involved: medicine, psychiatry, psychology, sociology, and education.

BORIS ZEMSKY, M.D.

Causation and Prevention of Emotional Difficulties in Reading

There is a definite connection between emotional disturbances and reading. Emotional disturbances rob us of energy needed for achievement in reading; our energy is used up in psychic mechanisms and operations. For example, many in this room, after a hard day at school when everything has happened, have gone home and said to a member of your family or your roommate, "I've had such a trying day I don't even know my own name." Here you see, emotional energy has been used up to such an extent that you are not able to use your intellectual potential. Similarly, emotional problems can rob a youngster of success in reading and other subjects. In a recent study done in California it was found that difficulty in reading and arithmetic is an early sign of emotional disturbances in children.

A large proportion of delinquent children are poor readers. Acting-out behavior problems and difficulty in reading usually go hand in hand. Reading difficulty also may be expressed psychosomatically, as in the case of youngsters who suddenly get a tummy ache or a headache or a backache and want to go to the nurse's office when they are called upon to read or spell. More severe are the personality, the neurotic, and even the pre-psychotic and the psychotic disturbances growing out of failure in reading. Among the drop-outs, too, there is a large proportion of poor readers.

How may these relationships be explained? What happened to the child? The child fears failure. We know what anxiety can do to any human being, most of all to a child. We have also been told how a child may be passively aggressive in handling his hostility toward a parent. Since the parent wants him to achieve in school, he does the opposite. The competitiveness of keeping up with his peer groups may also inhibit instead of stimulating some children.

Emotional disturbance associated with reading probably has two aspects. In some cases you have the child who, for many reasons, is a poor reader. This is frustrating to him. His self-esteem is lowered. Not having the proper tools to handle this frustration, he becomes emotionally disturbed. In other cases, we start with an emotional disturbance. This leads to poor reading because the child is using up psychic energy that should be devoted to learning to read.

Now what can we do about this? Here I'm going to do a little propagandizing and, I hope, add a little bit of provocative and stimulating thinking on my favorite subject – prevention. If we do nothing but sit here and talk, and if we wait until we have enough personnel to handle all the emotional problems, we will get nowhere.

We must stop and think about the role of the teacher in this problem. Teaching techniques can be used in the early identification of emotional problems and school difficulties that lead to later problems. I am emphasizing the role of teachers in the screening process. I am not interested in making therapists out of teachers. Teachers are not therapists. They are professionally trained as teachers; but they are important members of a team including psychologist, social worker, parent, administrators, businessmen, and others.

To handle the reading problem adequately we don't involve

just the child and the teacher. We have to involve the family because it is in the family that the child learns his attitudes, his values, and the psychological mechanisms with which he copes with his world. How can a child come to school and read if he is cold or hungry? How can a child learn how to read or spell if he has been up all night listening to mamma and papa fighting with each other, one or the other being intoxicated or physically abused?

So I am saying to you as a psychiatrist, as a doctor of medicine who practices this sub-specialty, we must look at the total person in a total social setting. We not only need some new techniques, we need also to train teachers to interview not only the child but the mother, the father, and any other important person in the child's environment. Personally I feel that if I had experience as a teacher, I would have been a better psychiatrist. It has taken me many years to learn how to conduct a psychiatric interview, and I am glad that those who have set up the Arizona International Reading Association have recognized the importance of interview techniques. In any interview setting, communication is of utmost importance – communication between mother and father, between parent and child, teacher and child, principal and teacher.

How do we communicate? Communication does not mean, as children have told me frequently, "yelling." You know, people have the idea that if you yell loud enough you will pound in the idea. This is not communication. Communication consists of many things – listening, looking for non-verbal clues, understanding, consideration, cooperation, empathy, and many more.

If teachers are not concerned with prevention, we're going to have more poor readers and more youngsters who are having emotional difficulties. Teachers must be interested not only in the three R's, but also in teaching and helping youngsters how to learn to live in the outside world with whatever abilities and assets they have.

RALPH D. RABINOVICH, M.D.

Neuropsychiatric Considerations in Children's Reading Problems

It is important to include the neuropsychiatric factors in a discussion of reading problems of children. As you know, there is an increasingly close relationship between our schools and our psychiatric clinics and hospitals for children. In our work in psychiatry, we are increasingly dependent on school people to help us in carrying on special educational programs for some of our disturbed children, and also in providing for them the special compensations, such as good relationships, that they need so much.

Another reality that we now face is the fact that a fair percentage of the children who come to our psychiatric clinics for study and treatment have reading problems. In recent years by far the largest single group of children who come to psychiatric clinics are referred by the schools, and a significant percentage of the boys in this group have reading difficulties. Of necessity, then, our multi-discipline workers here at Hawthorn Center have been obliged to become interested in the reading and language problems of children.

It is difficult to know for certain why so many children today have reading problems. The statistics of incidence, as you know, are unreliable. The reported figures range from 5 per cent of the children in some school populations all the way up to 20 per cent in others. In our work here we have the feeling that about 10 per cent of the children in most public school groups show a significant discrepancy between reading competence and mental age. Nationwide this represents a tremendously large number of children; it would actually run into the millions.

One of our major research interests has been to investigate the causes of reading problems. We have come to the general conclusion that three major groups can be defined among the total population of poor readers in our schools. First of all there are those children whose reading ability is impaired because of some as yet uncertain neurological deficit which prevents their dealing successfully with letters and words as symbols and thus limits their capacity to find meaning in written material. The problem here is a biologic or endogenous one and, therefore, we have called these cases primary reading retardation.

There is a second group of children who fail to learn to read because of brain damage that is manifested by clear-cut neurological disturbances. Here the history usually reveals the cause of the brain injury. Common agents are prenatal toxicity, birth trauma, anoxia or breathing difficulty at time of birth, encephalitis or infection of the brain, and, sometimes head injury. These cases, which are not very frequent, we call brain injury with resultant reading retardation.

The third group comprises children who have full capacity to learn to read but do not acquire or apply the skills of which they are capable. In other words, these children lack the reading techniques that would permit them to achieve a reading level commensurate with their intelligence. The causative factors here are exogenous or experiential; the child has a normal reading potential that, for a wide variety of reasons, has not been realized. There is no school teacher who does not know some of these children. Some are simply negative; they come to school with such a hostile attitude – usually directed at first towards the parents, then transferred to the teacher – that they will not learn. Some are so anxious about themselves or about their family relationships that their anxiety interferes with concentration and learning. Some may be depressed, and others are unable to evoke the kind of mental energy that is necessary for effective learning. Some are psychotic or mentally ill; fortunately they are not a very large group, but still they comprise a significant number. Others may be simply neglected – grossly unstimulated at home and, sometimes unfortunately, at school. Thus there is a wide range of external factors that may interfere with the reading achievement of children whose capacity to learn is intact, factors that prevent them from utilizing their capacity adequately. This whole group of children who are biologically intact we refer to as cases of secondary reading retardation.

This attempt at differential diagnosis we think has much more than academic interest. To meet a child's remedial needs, it is important that we try to determine the causative factors in his disturbance. The child whose language functions and reading capacity are intact but who does not learn because of emotional factors obviously needs some kind of special relationship, either within the classroom or in the school's special services. The emotional difficulty or personality factor that is interfering with his learning is the thing that requires attention. On the other hand, if the child has primary reading retardation caused by a neurological defect, his basic language functions are not intact and he really cannot translate symbols into meaningful concepts. All the psychotherapy or special relationships in the world will not help him to overcome his difficulty. Though there are no easy diagnostic tools available at the present time, we think our research is approaching a much more effective method of differential diagnosis.

At least we have reached the point in many cases where we can diagnose secondary reading retardation as associated with a bit of the primary syndrome. Through the years our group, and I believe many others, have come to view the incidence of the purely secondary retardations as lower than we at first anticipated. While the meaningfulness of what the child reads will be strongly conditioned by his life experience and personality, and while the rapidity of his progress in learning will be much influenced by his social opportunities, his basic mastery of symbolization is probably much more dependent on neurological factors than we once thought. I know that in some circles we are thought to be treading on dangerous ground when we say this, and in the best traditions of democratic education you should disagree with me if you feel you must.

This issue of the basic intactness of the child's language and learning capacity is most important. There has been a tendency for many workers to refer children with very severe reading problems to a psychiatric clinic with the expectation that the psychiatrist will trace the learning problem to an emotional block; through the magic of psychotherapy, perhaps after only a few interviews, the child will be released with the capacity to learn adequately. Unfortunately, I think that some of us in child psychiatry and clinical psychology have fostered this attitude in the past by over-generalizing dynamic factors. The problem is much more complex, and there is a need for a careful differential diagnosis in each case studied.

In recent years, educators have been placing a valid emphasis on content in learning, on the social meaningfulness of what is taught. This has led to many positive changes in curriculum. Repetitive drill work has been reduced in both language and arithmetic, much to the benefit of all school children. In the large majority of children, reading skills evolve spontaneously, stimulated and directed by good teachers. With these children, content becomes the major concern. Unfortunately, however, there are some for whom written material remains meaningless because they lack the technique of reading. There can be no content if there is no technique. The child in whom the process of symbolization is impaired has difficulty learning to translate letter symbols into concepts, no matter how skillfully he is motivated or how great an effort he makes.

The clinical picture in the primary reading retardation cases includes factors that tend to differentiate these cases from the secondary cases, those with simple emotional blocks or other exogenous factors that are interfering with learning. Let us start at the surface and work toward an understanding of primary disturbance in the reading process.

First, consider the level of reading retardation itself. In our primary cases, the disability is usually severe; apart from a small sight vocabulary, often learned by rote, and sporadic use of simple phonic skills, there may be almost no functional reading ability. Arithmetic competence, too, is usually low, although it may be somewhat higher than the reading level. The greatest impairment may be in spelling, as revealed when the child attempts to write from dictation.

Second, there is a disturbance in the reading process itself. Analysis of the child's reading performance indicates difficulties in both the visual and auditory areas; directionality also tends to be impaired. Visual recognition and discrimination on a perceptual level are intact, but the child cannot translate letter forms and combinations into meaningful concepts. In a similar way, in the auditory sphere differences in vowel sounds are appreciated when presented orally, but the child cannot translate the sounds into their letter symbols. For example, when a series of short vowel sounds – *a*, *e*, *i*, *o*, *u* – is presented orally, the child immediately recognizes the *a* as different from the *e*, but he cannot take the crucial step required for reading and spelling – the translation of the sound into its appropriate letter symbol. The difficulty, then, is in symbolization in both visual and auditory fields. To complicate the problem, the subject may also have left-right directional confusion with or without mixed laterality.

Third, we note broader language deficits, problems beyond the reading itself. While the child may appear to manage relatively well in everyday conversation, careful attention to his language pattern reveals frequent difficulty in specific name finding, in precise articulation, and in primitive syntax. The following are typical examples drawn from the responses made by severe primary cases to test questions.

A child is asked, "Why is it better to build a house of brick than of wood?" He replies, "Well, just in case a hurricane, the house can break down, but you put the brick on, it can just hit it but not break nothing down." This is a nine-year-old boy. Another question, "What must you do to make water boil?" A ten-year-old boy responds, "You should put it under a fire." An eleven-year-old boy is asked regarding a picture he has drawn, "How did he get hurt?" He replies, "He spranged a thing, an arm when he falled out of that tree." Another boy is asked, "Is it night time or day time now?" He replies, "Daytime, it's well, clouds are out and stuff. It's white the clouds. It lights them up. The clouds and stuff." These of course tend to be extreme examples. But we look for similar disturbances in expressive language in all cases of the primary syndrome.

Lastly, we think that children with primary retardation have a specific concept deficiency, especially with respect to orientation. Just as they have difficulty in translating sounds into their letter symbols, so they appear to have difficulty in translating orientational concepts into accepted symbols. Thus, while the child has no trouble appreciating which of two children is taller, he cannot define their height in feet. Similarly, while he knows clearly that he wakes up in the morning, he may be unable to express this knowledge in terms of a specific hour. To facilitate further exploration of this orientational factor, we devised at the Hawthorn Center a concept symbolization test comprising questions relating to personal information: time, quantity and dimension, number, directionality, and laterality. Our clinical psychologists are in the process of completing standardization of this test, which we hope may prove helpful as a diagnostic and prognostic instrument, especially with young children as a partial key to their need for therapy.

The disturbances in the reading process which I have outlined appear to be the most important differential diagnostic criteria. They are not found in children with neurotically or emotionally induced secondary reading retardations.

No discussion of neuropsychiatric factors in reading problems can avoid mention of the inordinate suffering experienced by otherwise normal children who are cut off from the communication channels that are increasingly vital for survival today. Since we have such meager resources for meeting their specific needs, we are obliged all too often to limit our involvement with them to documenting their successive psychological reactions – from initial anger to guilt feelings, to depression, and to ultimate resignation and/or modification of their aspirations. The spread of clinics throughout the country has encouraged us to hope that early intervention by well-trained language therapists may permit many children with primary reading retardation to develop at least functional reading competence.

Major needs are for early diagnosis and the provision of intensive remedial programs in the public schools. And may I say, a desperate need is to find facilities to help the classroom teacher spot these specific problems, and also to relieve her of the impossible responsibility of retraining the most severely disturbed. Another major need is for an adjusted curriculum throughout the school years that will rely only minimally on literacy. This must be devised for the sake of the students who will respond only minimally to corrective efforts.

It is interesting, if disconcerting, to note how much further advanced our speech correction programs are in comparison with those for reading therapy. It may be that speech correction workers have been more aggressive in presenting their reasonable demands and in the past have had more clear-cut programs to offer. However, now that reading diagnostic issues are becoming clarified and specific remedial techniques are evolving, the time is ripe for establishing large-scale, special reading services in our public schools. Such programs, financed by special appropriations that are now available in many states, must take their place alongside those already established for children with speech, visual, hearing, orthopedic, and other handicaps. In view of the fact that the public school is charged with no responsibility greater than that of teaching all children to read, the inclusion of remedial reading as a recognized branch of special education would seem as logical as it is essential.

DEMONSTRATED BY

LORA ANDERSON

Classroom Procedures with Emotionally Disturbed Children

THE GROUP

Three children were taught, one at a time, in demonstrating techniques which could be employed with a single child as he became increasingly competent in reading.*

OBJECTIVES AND PROCEDURES

In beginning work with an emotionally disturbed child, the teacher's objectives were:

1. To establish a good personal relationship and a pleasant, relaxed atmosphere.
2. To give the child a successful experience associated with reading.
3. To establish the child's self-confidence by checking informally on words that he had already learned.

*The children in the demonstration were eager to participate in the program and did not have severe emotional disturbances.

The teacher presented attractive pictures related to travel and discussed them with the child, calling attention to words pertaining to the subjects: *space*, *travel*, *jet*, *train*, *horse*, etc. They compared the different modes of travel with respect to speed, and the child arranged the pictures of vehicles from the fastest to the slowest. He also selected words he had already learned to read that described the pictures – *fast*, *slow*, *old*, *new*, etc. – and placed the printed words under the appropriate pictures.

With a slightly more advanced reader, the teacher encouraged the child to express his own ideas. She used the child's dictated story as a basis for reading instruction, calling attention to the importance of relating events in the correct order and of using an interesting vocabulary. The teacher read back the story the child had dictated and gave him opportunity to make any changes he wished to make.

As the child progresses further, the teacher planned

1. To give him practice in arranging in proper sequence sentences from short experience stories typed on separate cards.
2. To teach him ways of learning to read new words used in his experience stories.

Chapter Three

There are at least 22 million children and young people in the United States for whom English is a second language (10, p. 289). This figure represents roughly one person in eight. In the Southwest, the percentage is much higher. For example, in New Mexico nearly half the school-age children are handicapped to some degree because their parents do not speak English. Among these bilinguals are children whose ancestors have lived in the middle Rio Grande Valley for generations; children of Mexican-Americans who have recently crossed the border; children who speak the Keresan, the Tiwa, the Tewa, the Towa, and the Zuni languages of the Pueblo Indians; and

*"Bilingual" Children**

those who speak the Navajo and the Apache Athabaskan tongues. In addition the population includes occasional immigrant families from almost every country in the world. In recent years, Cuban refugees have been appearing on the scene with little or no knowledge of English. All these children must absorb English as they attend the elementary and secondary schools.

Many of these children are handicapped educationally, emo-

*"Bilingual" is used here as a convenient and commonly understood concept; as a matter of fact, many so-called "bilingual" children know only one language, and that imperfectly, when they come to school.

tionally, socially, and, later, vocationally by their inability to speak, write, and read English. Some become increasingly retarded in reading as they go through school; they develop feelings of inferiority and inadequacy. As a result, they often drop out of school prematurely or develop a hostility toward school and society. This handicap could be at least partially overcome by more effective instruction in the speaking, writing, and reading of the English language.

At present, many teachers lack understanding of the values and cultural patterns of these pupils, and of the depth of their linguistic difficulties. They also lack appropriate methods and materials of instruction.

There is need for a sound program that would take into account (1) the nature of the English language as described by linguists, (2) the relation between language and the culture of the people, as understood by anthropologists, (3) a sound psychological approach to the teaching of speech and reading to these cultural groups, (4) the successful procedures that have been developed by teachers who have worked with bilinquals of various ages and various cultural backgrounds, and (5) research on the actual process by which pupils learn English as a second language.

MAMIE SIZEMORE

Understanding "Bilingual" Children

The bilingual child has many of the problems that have already been mentioned, in addition to being linguistically handicapped. In the past, people have had the impression that all one needs to know to teach English as a second language is how to speak English. That is not true. Teachers must have a knowledge of the structure of the language. Naturally you would say, "Surely I know the structure of the English language. I've spoken it all my life." But do you?

From the child's viewpoint, the learning of English as a second language is not primarily an intellectual task. Vocabulary must be learned, to be sure; acquiring a fluency and correctness in speaking requires practice and more practice. The child who speaks the most English speaks the best English. As a teacher I used to have my boys with me, sometimes for as long as three years. Then they would go away to the army and come back in three months knowing more English than I had taught them in three years. Why? Because they had to use English in their daily living. This same approach has been used in teaching foreign languages to motivated adults. The linguistic approach is not a *method;* it is a growing body of knowledge and a scientific way of teaching a language.

The bilingual child has a tendency to hang on to his own sounds and his own sentence structures. In the New York City Puerto Rican study, it was helpful in the beginning to teach these children to speak Spanish. Many teachers do not agree with this point of view. We must remember, however, that we cannot teach a child to speak English in the same way that he has learned his native tongue. Why? Because he already has the means of communication and he cannot go back to his infantile methods.

Many teachers in Arizona are supplementing their basic reading program with special material to help children master the communication skills and become independent readers. They do not teach the phonetics of the language in a vacuum. Instead, they teach the sounds of the second language as an intrinsic part of the complete language arts program. Many teachers are able to achieve good results without the explicit aid of specific linguistic training, but by using newer methods they can do a much better job. The teaching of a second language is doomed to remain an amateur profession until we can bring about a scientific viewpoint gained by independent reading on this subject and by taking courses in the teaching of the communication skills to bilingual students.

Obviously the bilingual child needs to learn English sounds, some of which are not in his language. Experienced teachers of bilingual students who are learning English as a second language have found that their students need to learn to hear accurately and produce clearly the vowel and the consonant sounds.

What are we doing wrong in our classrooms? Why do we find capable second and third grade students doing failing work in the fourth, fifth, and sixth grades? Of course the differences in the social and cultural background and the economic status of the child enter in. But what can we do now in the schools before a long-range program to change these environmental conditions is carried out? Since language is the most typical, the most representative, and the most central element in any culture, and since language is the vehicle of the culture, how can we teach the child to adjust to another culture when he is not able to speak the language that is the vehicle of that culture?

When our primary children come to us, they accept English without relating it word by word to their own language and translating it into their native language, as the older children often do. When a child is small he may learn to speak a language more easily, perhaps because it comes entirely through the ear and not through the eye. He learns it by hearing and hearing and hearing. In school, bilingual young children will likewise learn the new language more easily through the ear than through the eye. Despite the pressure to put the children into books, into reading very quickly, I should like to see kindergartens for all bilingual children where we just teach the child to speak. I am glad to see programs where the child learns to read what he has spoken and then written.

Teachers of bilingual children have a great need for suitable instructional material, but I do not think that they should be expected to create material except experience charts and other material of special local interest. The creation of reading material is a job for many people: the classroom teacher, the linguist, the psychologist, and the person who can put it in the best literary form.

Finally, we must avoid putting labels on the Indian child and the Mexican-American child. I remember a lady came into my room one day and said, "Are they d-u-m-b?" And one little girl answered, "No, ma'am. Everyone of us can talk." Another little girl named Tita was very much aware of the social advantages of a wealthy classmate. One day she went home and told her mother, "I did a terrible thing today." Her mother asked, "What did you do?" She said, "Well, when we got to the end of the pledge of allegiance to the flag and they said 'justice for all,' I said, 'And justice for Tita, too.' " One of the most important ways of doing justice to our bilingual children is to help them acquire facility in reading and speaking English as their second language.

DR. MILES ZINTZ

Developing a Communication Skills Program for Bilinguals

The Indian research study recently completed at the University of New Mexico (18) concluded that there were four major obstacles to the more adequate teaching of boys and girls from minority ethnic groups in public schools.

1. The first obstacle to effective teaching of these pupils is the lack of understanding of the child to be taught. This necessitates understanding and appreciation of the life values, the cultural beliefs, motivations, and aspirations of the various minority ethnic groups. The cultural values described by the anthropologist, translated into a sociological frame of reference, provide this much-needed information for classroom teachers.

For example, middle-class school teachers have internalized values wherein the drive for achievement and success causes parents to "push" their children to climb the ladder of success, to work hard, to anticipate and to accept change, and to expect to take a considerable part in shaping their own future destinies. Pueblo Indian children most likely will be taught at home a harmony-with-nature rather than a mastery-over-nature philosophy; present-time orientation rather than future-time orientation; and a level of aspiration to follow in the ways of the old people. The traditional Spanish-American culture pattern places great value on "getting through this temporal life" so they may enjoy the rewards of the life hereafter; being satisfied with the present; the attitude in their villages is "work a little, rest a little."

A counterpart of this first need for understanding is a fairly clear revelation that most of us who are teaching have not really analyzed and understood our own life values, beliefs, and aspirations. In other words, many teachers are not aware of the middle-class values they hold, what their merits are, or in what ways minority groups may say objectively that they prefer their own traditional ways of life. This phase of the research suggests that teachers would certainly profit from orientation in sociology to better understand how behavior evolves and is controlled in social groups. They also need an orientation in cultural anthropology to better understand the contrasting, or even conflicting, social behavior of other groups with which they must interact.

It is at this point that the total interdependence of language and culture becomes evident. Language is an integral part of a people's culture. It is the way the heritage is transmitted. It is the means by which the attitudes and feelings of the group are made known. The only way accumulated experience can be recreated or interpreted is through language. Without language there would be no way of reviewing past experiences and communicating them to others.

2. The second major obstacle to better teaching of English as a second language is the language itself. Since English is the language of the school and, generally speaking, teachers are unilingual, the use of English by these bilingual children is the most conspicuous and probably the most fundamental problem.

The difficulties in translating concepts from one language to another are well known. Problems of cognate words that do not carry the same connotations in two languages have arisen in diplomatic circles. Saunders (12, pp. 111-117) emphasizes the differences in meanings beyond the literal translation of words from Spanish to English. For example, in English one says he missed the bus; in Spanish he says the bus left him. Language – for example, saying that dishes break by falling away from people and objects lose themselves – may reveal the way people in a culture view a given value, such as responsibility (12,- p. 117). In English the clock *runs;* in Spanish it *walks;* in French it *marches;* in German it *functions.*

Special problems are sure to arise in teaching a new set of language patterns against a background of different, even conflicting, native language or cultural habits. Lado (8, p. v) states that one of the chief difficulties is that the child has learned not only to attend to certain stimuli as cues to his responses, but also to ignore all those features which did not have a function in his own language. These blind spots may be exactly those features which do have signalling value in the second language.

3. The third major obstacle to better reading instruction is that schools have not initiated and developed systematic, planned courses of study in the learning of English as a second language. A consistent effort on the part of the total school system is needed to teach the common speech utterances of the language and to provide sufficient drill for habituation to the level of completely spontaneous use. Vocabulary concepts in the second language must be extended beyond the initial levels required by common, everyday speech. And, finally, the reading and writing of the language will be developed. Judged by the criteria of present-day second language teaching, we have been guilty in the past of starting first grade children with writing and reading when they do not have a sufficient background in speaking.

Teaching English as a second language requires an elementary knowledge of comparative linguistics. Teachers should be cognizant of the phonemes that appear in one language and not in the other, and ones that will be new and difficult to produce correctly in the second language. The natural result without specific teaching is for any speaker to substitute one of the familiar phonemes of his vernacular for a new phoneme which he has never learned. Word order in sentences varies with the language. While there are not radical differences in sentence patterning in Spanish and English, these differences are more extreme in a verb language like Navajo and a noun language like English. We may accept the logical fact that most teachers of these children will not become bilingual, but it would be possible for them to learn some of the linguistic differences in the two languages.

In the course of the Indian Research Study mentioned earlier (18, pp. 112-136) tests were devised to measure the vocabulary abilities of Spanish-speaking and Indian children. Semantic difficulties as found in common idiomatic expressions, multiple meanings of common words, simple analogies, and opposites were investigated. The study of difficulties children encounter with idioms was reported in the *Reading Teacher* (19). Four master's theses (4, 6, 9, 16) indicated that Indian and Spanish-American children are significantly handicapped in comparison with Anglo children with whom their performances were compared. The superiority of fourth grade Anglo children with unilingual backgrounds was statistically significant as compared with Indian and Spanish-American sixth grade children on all these tests.

The following are samples of some of these difficulties with English usage.

First, *understanding the idiom.* These idioms, in context, were taken from commonly used elementary school fourth, fifth, and sixth grade readers.

Mother will *piece out* the supper.
Tom knew he was *saved by a hair.*
His plan *fell through.*
"O.K.," he retorted. "*Don't bite my head off.*"
Mr. Bird chuckled, "Now I've *let the cat out of the bag.*"

Generally, children for whom English was the second language interpreted the idioms in a completely literal sense.

Second, *understanding commonly used slang expressions in the English language* is expected in ordinary conversation outside of school. For example:

Mr. Jones really *cramps my style.*
When everyone else quit, I was *stuck with the job.*

He is great for *talking through his hat.*
It's about time to quit fooling around and *talk turkey.*
Tom likes to *pull your leg* every chance he gets.

Third, *understanding all the uses of a single English word* is one of the greatest difficulties emphasized by Fries (5, pp. 38-56). "Run" has some seventy-five uses as given in the dictionary. Some examples are:

The boy will run a race.
The disease has run its course.
The fence runs east and west.
The man runs a garage.
The boy has run a splinter in a finger.
He will run out of money.
He will run up a bill.
He may run across an old friend.
He can knock a home run.
There was a run on the bank.
He is not the common run of person. (7, pp. 398-399)

Children for whom English is a foreign language are sure to have great difficulty with multiple meanings. A multiple choice test was devised, asking children to identify the *incorrect* use of a word. Sentences using the words *hold* and *left* will illustrate this type of test:

Don't hold me.
Look in the hold of the ship.
The cup can hold water.
Your clothes are full of hold.

And the word *left:*

He hurt my left hand.
There is nothing left.
We put left in the pan.
We left the city.

A fourth difficulty is the child's lack of adequate word meanings for words heard orally. Tireman found that children may completely misunderstand the word given when they attempt to use it orally in sentences (15, pp. 33-35).

Word given	*Sentence composed by child*	*Child's misconception*
blot	Where blood comes	(clot)
spool	A place where there is water	(pool)
tasks	They cut the tasks of the elephant	(tusks)
climate	The natives climate the trees to get coconuts	(climbed up)
oyster	A kind of bird in the zoo	(ostrich)

Fifth, simple analogies readily understood by Anglo fourth grade pupils give much difficulty to those for whom English is a second language. For example:

Water is to drink as bread is to *eat.*
Cowboy is to horse as pilot is to *plane.*
Tree is to trunk as flower is to *stem.*

4. The fourth major obstacle to learning English as a second language is serious educational retardation. This also must be met and overcome. The work of Tireman (14, pp. 45-50), Singer (13, pp. 3-10), Sanchez (11), Coombs (2), and Boyce (1) has shown a general tendency for pupils to become more and more educationally retarded as they progress through the schools; many of these students either drop out or become hopelessly lost in the high school.

Current testing reinforces the previous findings that as children from minority ethnic groups progress through the school grades their achievement falls farther and farther behind. Not only are they from one to two years over-age for their grades, on the average, but they also are educationally retarded an additional one to two years in achievement on standardized tests.

In the *Navajo Yearbook* (17), Young has also emphasized that one of the major problems in the field of Navajo education is that of educational retardation. This educational retardation made itself strongly felt with the transfer of Indian children to public schools. Public school personnel were concerned that

Navajo children accepted for enrollment be "up to grade." Of 9,751 children whose records were analyzed in December, 1957, only 6 per cent were "up to grade," 40 per cent were retarded at least one year, and 54 per cent were retarded two or more years (17).

It is apparent from data obtained in 1960 that there continues to be one full year of over-ageness for these minority ethnic groups. This is not as significant, however, as the fact that, even though the sample children were over-age in grade, they were an additional one and one-half to two years retarded in achievement as measured by a survey reading test. Over-ageness and retardation must be added together to determine the full extent of educational retardation. This severity of educational retardation follows the same pattern recognized by Sanchez, Tireman, and Sininger three decades previously.

Against the child's total language arts experience, two general comments about the process of reading itself should be mentioned.

The first comment relates to teaching word-attack skills programs to second-language children. The phonetic approach to words is apt to be less helpful to the child than we may at first realize. He does need to know how to pronounce the word, but the usefulness of phonetic analysis to him is limited when he does not know the meaning of the word. Teachers in elementary schools in Mexico City have reported that they have no difficulty teaching first grade children to read the daily newspaper since the Spanish language is so completely phonetic, but they must spend all the rest of the elementary school years teaching them to understand what they read! Actually, they have not really taught these children to *read;* they have only taught a word-calling process.

Tireman wrote that phonetic and structural analysis are useful to the English-speaking child who has an adequate oral vocabulary. When he analyzes a word he recognizes its meaning when he hears himself say it. However, for the non-English-speaking child, who has a limited oral vocabulary, phonetic and structural analysis is less helpful (15).

The second comment relating to the reading process is that, by now, it must be clear that *meaningful concepts* is the most important goal to be attained. Teachers must continually work on concepts. Children develop meanings through experiencing the concept in many different ways. First-hand experiences, visual aids, dramatizations, and *practice*, *practice*, *practice* are essential in a long-range program of developing greater skills in all the language arts. Reading is an intrinsic part of the language arts hierarchy of listening and speaking skills competently developed.

A second grade teacher of unilingual children described how she discussed with and elicited from her class a variety of responses concerning meanings of the word *track*. The number of different meanings introduced at one time will depend upon the experiences of the boys and girls.

> The word track was being discussed in the classroom in connection with a story regarding street cars. Some of the children had never seen a street car and so Bill, a city boy, said that they were cars that ran by electricity on tracks. When asked to describe what a track looked like, he said it was a long steel thing that ran in two lines down the middle of the street. John, the "desert rat," with a puzzled look on his face, wanted to know what kind of tracks the car made. We got to talking about the words that looked the same but meant different things, and it was suggested that each child tell what the word *track* meant to him.
>
> Sharon said that many times her mother told her not to track up the clean kitchen floor. To her it meant to get something dirty. Melinda mentioned that she had heard her father discuss the sound track of his tape recorder. Steve contributed the fact that his father tracked a missile on a tracking board. Peter mentioned the new race track outside El Paso. Joe told of riding on a train which ran on tracks and how the wheels made a clicking sound as they went over the joints in the tracks. John told of the time he had found coyote tracks in the snow and had tracked them to the boundary lines of the Post. Bruce, the slow-

> poke of the class, said that his mother had told him to 'make tracks' for school that morning. "She meant me to hurry up," he said by way of explanation.
>
> By the time we were through, we had collected quite a few meanings for the word *track* and had learned a lesson in word comprehension. For, as one child expressed it, "You have to know what you are reading about to know what the word means." (3)

Finally, I should like to propose a problem for research: How proficient in the oral use of English must the bilingual child be before he can be expected to make progress in reading and writing it? The severely controlled vocabularies of beginning reading programs are no criterion for judging the speaking vocabularies of the children who learn English after they come to school. Typical middle-class Anglo children may have a *listening vocabulary* of between eight and ten thousand words and may use at least five thousand words in their *speaking vocabulary* when they come to school at age six. It becomes apparent that the Indian child taught 315 words in the pre-first grade program (following the Minimum Essential Goals) is hardly ready to begin the formal first grade reading program his second year in school.

If we had a systematic program of first teaching English as a second language and were willing to work for an extended program with oral and written language adapted to these children's needs and experiences, could we overcome the perpetual educational retardation which they experience in our public schools? Should these boys and girls spend three years in school studying English as a method of communication, with only enough reading included to meet the teacher's plan for introducing a wide variety of topics of interest? If they were sophisticated in their knowledge of spoken English and *then reading skills were developed sequentially from the beginning*, would they be able to make progress in reading much faster? Basically, we try to teach much too much, much too soon, and we never do take adequate stock of where the children have been left behind. Consequently we never do systematically help them to catch up.

A more mature ten-year-old child who has gained some mastery over the English language, which he needs to use every day, should make faster progress as a result of formal reading than the seven-year-old bilingual child. Nobody really knows whether it is reasonable to expect that children who learn English after beginning school should be able to progress through the elementary school in six years.

Some of us who have worked in remedial reading clinics have found boys and girls beginning fifth grade in public schools with normal intelligence but no ability to read. With adequate clinical teaching, they have developed a fifth or sixth grade level of reading ability by the end of the sixth grade. If these normally intelligent children can develop the reading skills over a two-year period of remedial instruction, why could we not expect comparable success with children for whom English is a second language if we spend an extended period of language teaching, bridge the gap caused by cultural differences, and provide many kinds of group experiences to make the textbooks they are required to read more meaningful?

In summary, I have suggested that in order to teach the bilingual child more successfully, we need (1) an increased understanding of his cultural values and beliefs, (2) an increased appreciation of the relationship of the language the child uses to his total cultural heritage, (3) sophistication in techniques in the teaching of English as a second language, and (4) systematic planning based on careful diagnosis for overcoming educational retardation. Many of the points made here are controversial. They should be evaluated by continued experience and experiment.

REFERENCES

1. Boyce, George. "Why Do Indians Quit School?," *Indian Education,* 344 (May 1, 1960).
2. Coombs, L. Madison *et al. The Indian Child Goes to School.* Washington, D.C.: U.S. Department of the Interior, 1958.

3. Day, Marjorie F., primary teacher, The White Sands Missile School, New Mexico.

4. Dudding, Christine. "An Investigation into the Bilingual Child's Comprehension of Antonyms." Unpublished Master's thesis, The University of New Mexico, Albuquerque, 1961.

5. Fries, Charles C. *Teaching and Learning English as a Second Language.* Ann Arbor: University of Michigan Press, 1947.

6. Hess, Stephen G. "A Comparative Study of the Understanding which Bilingual Students have of the Multiple Meanings of English Words." Research in progress, The University of New Mexico, Albuquerque, 1962.

7. Horn, Ernest. "Language and Meaning." *The Psychology of Learning.* Forty-first Yearbook, Part II, National Society for the Study of Education. Chicago: University of Chicago Press 1942.

8. Lado, Robert. *Linguistics Across Cultures.* Ann Arbor: University of Michigan Press, 1958.

9. Mercer, Veta W. "The Efficiency of Bilingual Children in Understanding Analogies in the English Language." Unpublished Master's thesis, The University of New Mexico, Albuquerque, 1960.

10. Pei, Mario. *The Story of Language.* Philadelphia: J. B. Lippincott, 1949.

11. Sanchez, George I. *The Age-Grade Status of the Rural Child in New Mexico Public Elementary Schools, 1931-1932.* Educational Research Bulletin, Vol 1. Santa Fe: Department of Education, November 1932.

12. Saunders, Lyle. *Cultural Differences and Medical Care.* New York: The Russell Sage Foundation, 1954.

13. Sininger, Harlan. "An Age-Grade Study of the San José Training School and its Two Control Schools." *San José Training School.* University of New Mexico Bulletin, School Series, Vol 1, No. 2. Albuquerque: University of New Mexico Press, 1931.

14. Tireman, Loyd S. *Teaching Spanish-Speaking Children.* Albuquerque: The University of New Mexico Press, 1948.

15. Tireman, Loyd S. "The Bilingual Child and his Reading Vocabulary." *Elementary English,* 32:33-35 (January 1955).

16. Yandell, Maurine D. "Some Difficulties which Indian Children Encounter with Idioms in Reading." Unpublished Master's thesis, The University of New Mexico, Albuquerque, 1959.

17. Young, Robert W. *The Navajo Yearbook, 1958*, Report No. VII. Window Rock, Ariz.: The Navajo Agency, 1958.

18. Zintz, Miles V. (director). *The Indian Research Study: The Adjustment of Indian and non-Indian Children in Public Elementary Schools in New Mexico*. Sponsored under a grant from the U.S. Office of Education, Cooperative Research Branch, 1957-1960. Albuquerque: The College of Education, The University of New Mexico.

19. Zintz, Miles V. and Yandell, Maurine. "Some Difficulties Which Indian Children Encounter with Idioms in Reading," *The Reading Teacher*, 14:256-259 (March 1961).

DEMONSTRATED BY

JANE MOORE

Classroom Procedures with "Bilingual" Children

The Class

First grade children, eight girls and 16 boys, 19 of whom are bilingual. Eleven of these pupils are attending school for the first time this year; seven were in a pre-first grade in which facility in oral communication as a prelude to instruction in reading was emphasized; six are repeating the first grade. As measured by the Metropolitan Readiness Test and the Lorge-Thorndike Intelligence Test, the group was below average.

The pupils had been busy making and carrying out plans for the First Grade Orientation program. This event is held each spring for children who will be entering school the following September. During the Orientation Day, some of the preschool children spent part of the morning in the classroom. Among the visitors were brothers and sisters of pupils in the first grade class.

Specific Objectives and Illustrations of Procedures

1. To encourage spontaneous and voluntary communication through personal questions such as: Who is absent in your group? Do you know why he is absent? And through questions about their experiences:

T. What happened last week? Do you remember, Pablo?
P. We had visitors?
T. Who came?
P. Our brothers and sisters, and our visitors played with our clay. (The children read from the teacher's chart the story they had previously written:)

Our Visitors

We expect 10 visitors. They will come on April 5.
Some will be our brothers. Some will be our sisters.
They will be first graders.

T. We wrote a song for our visitors. What was the name of the song?
P. "Our Song for You."
T. What does "you" stand for?
P. Our visitors.
T. Would you like to sing it now?
(Pupils sing the song they wrote)
We are happy to see you today
We hope you have fun with our clay.
Here is a pretty hat for you.

2. To introduce and enrich children's vocabulary through relating their first-hand, meaningful, and personal experiences. New words such as *visitors*, *cookies*, *refreshments* were introduced in the conversation.

3. To see the relation between spoken word and written symbol by writing on the board some of the sentences the children dictated during their discussion:

T. Let's write a story about our visitors. Who has thought of a first line?

P. My friend played with the clay.
T. Yes, your little friend played with the clay. Did he have a good time, Joseph?
P. He said, "Thank you for the cookies and the punch."
T. He is a very polite boy, isn't he? What did your visitor like best, Juanita?
P. She liked the clay and hats and school. She didn't want to go home. Mrs. Moore, I told my sister she could come to school next year and she said she wanted to come now.
T. I'm glad our visitors liked school. That would make a good first line for our story. (Writes: Our visitors liked school.) What else did they like?
P. Our hats and our clay.
P. Cookies and punch.
P. Our song
T. (Writes: Our visitors liked our song, hats, and clay.) How many visitors did we have?
P. Six.
T. (Writes: Six visitors came to school.)
(Class reads the story:) Six visitors came to school. Our visitors liked school. They liked our song, hats, and clay.

In writing an experience chart, the teacher tries to select a central idea, makes sentences short and related to one another, and repeats words and phrases to insure learning.

4. To teach children to recognize basic sight words: *school*, *liked*, *they*, are several additional key words in the experience stories.

T. I see a word on the first line and the same word on the third line. Who can find it?
P. (Goes to board and frames the word *school* in both lines.)
T. And another word in both lines?
P. (Frames *visitor*.)

T. Who can find another word that is used in two sentences?
P. (Frames *liked.*)
T. Let's read the first line of our story. (Also uses phrase and sentence cards to match with sentences on board or chart.)
P. (Read: Our visitors like school.)
T. What else did they like?
P. (Read: They liked our song, hats, and clay.)
T. How many visitors came to school?
P. (Read: Six visitors came to school.)
T. Are *come* and *came* the same? What letter is different? Josephine, *come* to me. (Child approaches teacher then goes back to her seat.)
Josephine *came* to me.

5. To give opportunity for fluent oral expression through choral speaking:
T. What special day is coming soon?
P. Easter.
T. Shall we say the poem about the bunnies? What is the name of the poem?
P. "Song of the Bunnies" (by Margaret Wise Brown).
T. Who begins speaking – boys or girls?
P. Girls.
T. And who speaks alone?
P. Juanita.
(Class gives the choral speaking of the poem. Teacher notes several persistent mispronunciations which she will work on later.)

6. To build the concept of time – day and month:
T. Who can tell me what day today is?
P. Today is Friday.
T. Now who remembers what month it is?
P. March.
T. Last month was March. This month is ———.
P. April.

T. Yes, this month is April. And what day is it? Yesterday was April 5. Today is April ———.

P. Six.

T. Who remembers the year?

P. 1962.

T. And what was the weather when you came to school this morning?

P. Sunny and warm.

T. Now we are ready to write our weather report. (Writes it on board.) Today is Friday,
April 6, 1962
It is sunny and warm.

(Pupil reads the weather report.)

T. Very clear and accurate. Now let's have everybody read it.

7. To reinforce habits of courtesy by teacher's example and by approving and commenting on courteous behavior of pupils.

Questions and Comments

Should bilingual children stay in the first grade for two years? Many need two years to learn to speak English before they are given instruction in reading. If the state permitted, these children would profit by entering school at five years of age. They are put into books too soon. Parents often demand it. We need to help parents understand what is the best reading program for their children.

How do you handle three groups within the first grade? One group is busy with work sheets pertaining to their lesson or with following directions on the board; an advanced group is reading books and playing reading games, while the teacher gives instruction in reading to the third group. If a child finishes his work sheet before the others, he may get a "fun" book or mimeographed exercise sheet from the desk.

Should bilingual children be put together in a 1-C class, a section of the first grade where they are given instruction and much practice in speaking English? Does segregation of this kind have any detrimental psychological effect on the child?

If the child comes to school wanting to learn to read and write and, instead, spends the time in playing and oral English activities, he and his parents may feel disappointed. In one school the bilingual children seem to have no feeling of being different. There are seven first grades, one of which is a 1-C class. All the children are together on the playground.

Other ways of building a foundation of oral vocabulary and sentence structure before beginning to teach reading are: (1) having a group of bilingual children within a regular first grade class, (2) establishing kindergartens, or (3) having a summer school in which bilingual children have six to eight weeks of preparation before entering first grade. Much of the failure in the fifth and sixth grades may stem from poor methods of teaching English in the primary grades. Beginners need much emphasis on natural speaking in sentences and phrases. Unless they acquire basic language patterns and correct pronunciation early, when they reach the seventh and eighth grades they tend to become more and more reluctant to talk and more hostile to school and society.

Are there any programs for helping non-English-speaking pupils in the upper grades? In Tucson, Betty Frey has been using the aural-oral approach for three periods a week with seventh grade pupils who come from Mexico and cannot speak English. For next year, pilot projects are planned in two junior high schools. We cannot give these older non-reading pupils books about Dick and Jane. They must have experiences on their intellectual level. At present there is very little suitable reading material. To prepare such material is one of our most important problems.

There should be a coordinated program beginning in the elementary school and continuing through junior high school. Such a program would prevent many unnecessary drop-outs who, in this country as a whole, constitute one-third of the students who go to high school. Many of them drop out because they have not had the right kind of experiences in learning to read and *enjoy* reading. The schools are beginning to be interested in working with adults as well as with children.

Chapter Four

The mentally retarded are usually described as children whose intelligence as measured by an individual intelligence test is between sixty and eighty I.Q. However, there are several reasons why we are becoming more and more dissatisfied with this definition. In the first place, no important decision should be based on a single test; an intelligence test only shows how the person is functioning at the time, under the particular testing conditions. In individual cases, test results have differed from one test to another by as much as forty points. No pupil should be placed in a special class or school for the mentally retarded until he has been carefully observed under favorable school conditions for at least a year.

Moreover, an analysis of the test results almost always shows an irregular profile. The individual who scores below average in some of the subtests will almost certainly score above average in others; the scores are seldom uniformly low. The high points indicate potentialities that are above the level commonly associated with mental deficiency.

A careful examination of the child and his developmental his-

The Mentally Retarded

tory often indicates that he is not physiologically retarded, but rather comes from a retarded home or school. His mental growth curve as measured by tests is not his true developmental curve. If we can change the conditions that are blocking or depressing his mental growth, the child may be freed to follow his natural growth trend.

Teachers too often assume that an I.Q. below eighty on a child's record means that he will not make much progress in reading. Yet it has been reported that preschool children who were diagnosed as mentally deficient have been taught to read by using the electric typewriter, and that adolescents with I.Q.'s of fifty to sixty have learned to read well enough to get and hold appropriate jobs.

No one method will be successful with all cases. One individual learns by one method; another will succeed better with another method. More important than any specific method is clear, concrete instruction, reading material with which the individual can succeed, and an atmosphere of acceptance and optimism.

MARY BARRECA

Identification of and Programs for the Mentally Retarded

Fortunately, today teachers are well aware of individual differences in children. They are concerned about the little fellows who either sit back in a corner of the room and try to hide, or are boisterous in their attempts to cover up for their individual inadequacies.

And what does the teacher usually do? He probably first looks over the information available in a cumulative record booklet and consults the principal about the procedures that should be used. The next step is usually to refer an individual for psychological evaluation. In my school district all the testing is done by the Department of Counseling and Guidance. Each teacher submits to the guidance office as much background information as possible on any youngster who is being referred. Sometimes we think, "What's the use of all this information?" But it is extremely vital to the psychologist who is going to do the testing.

After the psychological evaluation is made, if it has been determined that the child is mentally retarded, the next step is to try to place the child in a special education class. Placement is not always done immediately. There are many children awaiting placement, because of lack of classroom space. Today in our district alone there are approximately two hundred and fifty. Placement is made on an individual basis. Conferences are held with the parents so that they completely understand the problem; also, the youngster's interests and abilities are considered before he is placed in any special education classroom. Many times a youngster may travel across town to a class completely out of his own district. Why? Simply because the supervisor feels that a particular teacher would be best for that individual child.

When a mentally retarded child with an I.Q. of sixty enters school at six years of age, he is only approximately three years, seven months old mentally. When he is seven years of age, he is four years and two months; when eight, four years and ten months; at nine, five years and five months; and at ten, approximately six years of age mentally and ready for the first grade. What happens to these children? Where do they go? In Tucson District No. 1 we have four educational levels for the mentally retarded: the primary level is for boys and girls between the chronological ages of six and nine, and the intermediate level for boys and girls between the ages of ten and twelve. These two groups are housed in elementary schools all over the city. Children between the ages of thirteen and sixteen are on the third or advanced level. These classes are in our junior high schools. The fourth or vocational level, including youngsters between the ages of sixteen and eighteen, is housed at the J. Howenstein School; this is the only segregated school program we have.

What kind of reading program should be offered to the mentally retarded? On this question there are two schools of thought. There are those who truly feel that the mentally retarded child does not need and cannot profit by any kind of reading program. There are others who feel that each of these children has a potential reading ability that we should help him develop. I belong to the latter school.

It is very important, however, that the reading instruction

given to the mentally retarded be practical and vital. That is why we delay any formal reading instruction until these children reach the intermediate level at ten or twelve years of age. At this time they are introduced to reading, but it is not of a "Dick and Jane" variety because many of our children do not belong to the culture of Dick and Jane; furthermore, they are very bored with the goings and comings of Dick and Jane, particularly if they have been exposed to these basal readers in regular classrooms. Therefore we try to find new interesting material built on their everyday experiences. To interest these pupils in reading, special education teachers use many types of stories, field trips, and visual aids. The teacher's greatest concern is that the mentally retarded first learn to read certain signs and directions that they find in their immediate environment and in the city.

At the advanced level when most of the boys and girls are approaching their maximum capacity, we stress reading in their various subjects. If any formal academic training is to be given, this is the place to do it.

On the vocational level, which is usually terminal education for these young people, our reading program is based on the everyday use they are going to make of their acquired skills, uses such as reading the newspapers and the want ads, or the filling out of application blanks. They also need to be able to read something about insurance, taxes, social security, and other things they will hear about. They should know about different kinds of jobs and qualifications for them. The reading program should teach mentally retarded boys and girls what they can learn and what they will make use of now and later. Education of the mentally retarded is for living and for livelihood.

DR. NORRIS G. HARING

Teaching Reading to Mentally Retarded Children

We shall focus our attention here upon specific psychological characteristics either directly or indirectly related to reading. Among these we shall include: (a) disorders of perception; (b) poor eye-hand coordination and gross motor coordination; (c) handedness, sightedness, directionality and laterality; (d) hyperactivity and short attention span; (e) poor discrimination in auditory and other sensory systems; (f) difficulty in associating sound with symbol or symbol with sound; and (g) poor retention of words previously learned.

Importance of Diagnosis

It is not reasonable to assume that the same approach to teaching reading is equally appropriate to all children who are classified as mentally retarded. By determining the cause of the retardation we gain important clues to the approach we should take in teaching. Cruickshank (1), Werner (13), Strauss and Lehtinen (12), and Strauss and Kephart (11) have said that children with brain injuries require special methods of training. Kephart (5) and Delacato (2) have worked out specific motor sequences for children with developmental irregularities. It has also been demonstrated that gross etiological classifications have some value in indicating appropriate teaching methods. In any case, there is sufficient evidence to support the assertion that ideally the teacher of the mentally retarded should approach the teaching of reading only after he has given specific diagnostic attention to the child's developmental status. Reading is a developmental process which begins long before the child actually realizes that symbols have meanings. It is a sophisticated process involving a complex integration of perception, visual and auditory discrimination, concept formation, motor coordination, and visual maturity.

Mentally retarded children are backward in reading owing to one or more of the following causes: disordered functioning or arrested development, extreme deprivation of stimuli in their environment, pathology or injury to the brain, and emotional disorders. Significant retardation in many areas of development is usually associated with retardation in reading. For the most part, the mentally retarded child is not ready for the usual reading program until one to three years after his normal peers.

A Sequence of Activities Contributing To Reading

The methods to be followed in teaching a mentally retarded child are to be determined by his developmental status. In presenting a reading program for mentally retarded children from the primary level to the junior high level, we shall restrict our recommendations to a sequence of activities that directly involve reading. It should be remembered, however, that language activities and many other kinds of experiences not mentioned here have an important influence on reading.

1. *Training perception and eye-hand coordination:* Our first consideration, regardless of the child's age on entering the program, is to determine his ability to distinguish forms such as circles, squares, and triangles. To strengthen this ability we use activities that involve the sorting of color and form. The child is asked to sort dominoes according to their color, and to sort

large nursery beads according to form and color. He may learn to distinguish additional shapes by using parquetry blocks and paper forms made from colored construction paper.

Quite a wide variety of puzzles can be made by teachers. These should be simple – two or three pieces that form a single object such as a face, bottle, animal, letter, or number. The child can move from teacher-made puzzles to commercial jigsaw puzzles.

A variety of stencils made from heavy cardboard are used to develop the child's skill in coloring within a frame. As the child learns to color within the frame, one side of the stencil is removed, then another, until the stencil is entirely removed and the child can color within lines without the aid of a stencil.

Colored designs made of paper are taped to 4 x 4 inch pegboards. If the child has difficulty reproducing a design on the pegboard, he may be asked to draw it on paper first. The designs are varied and gradually become more difficult. Colored one-inch cubed counting blocks are also used for practice in block design. Colored one-inch paper squares mounted on cardboard may also be used. The child places the cubes on the design. Here, too, the child makes a variety of designs.

Sorting and matching pictures, letters, and numbers are additional activities to develop the child's ability to discriminate. A large card of pictures is made, and the child places his individual pictures on the matching pictures of the card. Similar material in reading readiness workbooks may also be used.

Letters and numbers can next be differentiated. The teacher puts letters or numbers into the same group, using only as many items as the child can handle. The child separates the letters from the numbers. Next the child sorts letters according to all the colors – the green *a's*, the red *b's*, the orange *c's*, and so on for each letter or number. Then the child identifies letters that are all black.

Finally, the child can be asked to reproduce various designs by memory. For example, simple signs are presented and then taken away.

Cutting helps to develop the child's ability to coordinate eye and hand. A cutting sequence can begin by using two pieces of cardboard as guides. First the child cuts in a straight line with one piece of cardboard. Then he cuts geometric figures made with heavy straight lines, such as squares and triangles. After this he cuts heavy curved lines and circles and very simple pictures outlined with a heavy line. Gradually he works up to more complex pictures.

2. *Developing gross motor activities:* Research I have recently conducted on remedial physical activities involving gross motor integration has revealed a low, but significant, correlation between gains in reading and gains in gross motor activities. Similarly, other research has shown a positive correlation between gross motor integration and the reading process. Although we cannot assume that this is a cause-and-effect relationship, it is nonetheless important enough to suggest that a motor training program be used in connection with reading. These are some of the activities included in the motor training program: Walking a board, identifying body parts, imitating movements, running an obstacle course, making "angels in the snow," using stepping stones, and chalk board activities.

3. *Teaching phonics:* When the child has developed proficiency in the areas discussed so far, he has reached a developmental level which makes it possible for him to succeed in perceiving symbols and learning their sounds. At this point he can find success and enjoyment in matching words with objects and in building words. A basic reading vocabulary is built by varied repetition in meaningful context. Through reading charts, the child confronts a wider variety of words that are already in his speaking vocabulary. As he meets unfamiliar words, he must learn ways to attack them.

A concrete system of phonics should be selected. The phonovisual system (9) has the advantage of being based on linguistic principles and representing the sounds visually by concrete objects as well as by symbols. There are several other satisfactory phonics systems. The method which Kirk (6) describes in his book suggests the use of the Kirk-Hegge drills. Fernald (3) pays particular attention to tactual reinforcement. The Science Research Associates Reading Laboratory also has possibilities for use with the mentally retarded.

Mentally retarded children have unique learning needs. It is not unusual to find such children with language disabilities in both reading and speaking. Serious visual and auditory perceptual problems are frequently present among these children. The kinds of activities that we have described have been developed on the basis of our knowledge of the neurological organization and development of the child. This is not a new idea by any means. Seguin (10) expressed this notion about a hundred years ago. Some forty years later Montessori (7, 8) developed an elaborate set of materials that were originally designed for mentally retarded children. Montessori's basic assumptions about early sensory training were sound, but her approach should be re-examined with particular reference to the mentally retarded. Her materials have not been modified a great deal over the years.

4. *Reading experience charts:* It is good to keep in mind that the mentally retarded child finds reading easier and more meaningful when a word plays a functional part in his daily experience. This result is attained through use of the experience unit. The following sequence of activities is an example of the way an experience or a reading experience unit is initiated.

The experience is introduced to the group, and is followed by discussion. In the discussion the children mention pertinent facts, which are listed on the board. From the phrases and sentences thus dictated, the children develop a story which the teacher writes. The pupils read the story and copy it in their booklets. Words that are new, generally useful, and necessary to the unit are presented on flash cards. These newly learned words are listed with words learned previously. They are also written on the chalkboard and pronounced by the class. This story is typed with a primary typewriter and cut into short phrases and words which the pupils rebuild into a connected story.

With the mentally retarded, retention is a problem. To fix a word or idea in mind, the child is given many exposures to it;

these involve visual, auditory, tactual, kinesthetic, and even olfactory stimulation. The experience unit provides a natural opportunity for using all the sensory systems as means to learning. This approach can be broadened to include any subject. Since some mentally retarded children, particularly those with brain injury, require more structure in the beginning of their educational experiences, the experience unit is not so effective in these cases as a structured, stimuli-reduced environment.

At the junior high age, the teacher of educable, mentally handicapped children is still concerned with basic reading skills. The content of their reading material, however, should be appropriate to their adolescent interests. The experience unit is still an effective method; it follows the same form but varies in content. It provides for the necessary repetition as well as for individual interests and instruction.

The process that leads toward reading is an orderly one. With mentally retarded children, reading activities are too often introduced ahead of the developmental status of the child. With these children, the reading process often lags two or three years behind that of the average child.

Concluding Statement

In summary, let us review the characteristics of mentally retarded children, the implications of these characteristics for the reading process, and the sequence to be followed in teaching reading.

Among mentally retarded children, one may expect to find the following traits that affect reading: distortion in the sensory processes; lack of both fine and gross motor coordination; vaguely defined self concepts and body image; short attention span; and an apparent lack of interest, motivation, and curiosity which is frequently reflected in a lack of energy and enthusiasm. The opposite of this last characteristic occurs in hyperactive children who seem to have excessive energy but are incapable of controlling it or of channeling it in constructive ways.

The characteristics of the retarded child require specific modifications in the typical reading program. Specific attention must be paid to sensory training and motor coordination. A structured reading sequence is essential. Very rarely will one find a retarded child who has learned to read by chance; he requires a concrete and efficient system of phonics with considerable reinforcement, a great deal of practice, and immediate evaluation and correction. The reading material must be drawn from or refer to meaningful, functional life experiences.

In the preschool and primary years – that is, at chronological ages four to nine – the reading program should concentrate on sensory training, language skills, and motor coordination. This focus should be continued throughout the intermediate level, ages nine through twelve. At this level the following activities are added: readiness activities; experience with matching and building words; strengthening of the sight vocabulary; concentration on word attack skills; and numerous meaningful reading experiences. On the junior high level, all the preceding activities are reinforced and the scope of the content is greatly extended. Many projects that require reading are introduced. The use of reading as an important practical tool is emphasized.

There is much more detail which should be supplied in this presentation. Each mentally retarded child offers his own unique learning charactertistics that must be recognized and provided for.

References

1. Cruickshank, William M., Frances A. Bentzen, Frederick H. Ratzeburg, and Miriam T. Tannhauser. *A Teaching Method for Brain-Injured and Hyperactive Children.* Syracuse, New York: Syracuse University Press, 1961.
2. Delacato, Carl H. *The Treatment and Prevention of Reading Problems.* Springfield, Ill.: Charles C. Thomas, 1959.
3. Fernald, Grace M. *Remedial Techniques in Basic School Subjects.* New York: McGraw-Hill, 1943.
4. Gillingham, Anna and Bessie W. Stillman. *Remedial Training for*

Children with Specific Disability in Reading, Spelling and Penmanship. New York: Sackett and Wilhelm Lithograph, Inc., 1960.

5. Kephart, Newell C. *The Slow Learner in the Classroom.* Columbus, Ohio: Charles E. Merrill Books, Inc., 1960.
6. Kirk, Samuel O. *Teaching Reading to Slow Learning Children.* Boston: Houghton Mifflin Company, 1940.
7. Montessori, Maria. *The Montessori Method.* New York: Frederick A. Stokes Company, 1912.
8. Montessori, Maria. *The Absorbent Mind.* Madra 20, India: 1949.
9. Phono-Visual Products, Inc., 4803 Wisconsin Ave., N.W., Washington 16, D.C.
10. Seguin, Edward. *Idiocy and Its Treatment by the Physiological Method.* New York: Columbia University Press, 1907.
11. Strauss, Alfred A. and Newell C. Kephart. *Psychopathology and Education of the Brain-injured Child.* Vol. II. New York: Grune and Stratton, 1955.
12. Strauss, Alfred A. and Laura E. Lehtinen. *Psychopathology and Education of the Brain-injured Child.* Vol. I. New York: Grune and Stratton, 1947.
13. Werner, Hans. "Development of Visuo-motor Performance on the Marble-board Test in Mentally Retarded Children," *J. Genet. Psych.*, 64:1944.

DEMONSTRATED BY

FRANK GUNTER

Classroom Procedures with Mentally Retarded Children

The Class

In this class, with an age range of from eight to fourteen, there are mentally retarded, brain-injured, emotionally disturbed, and hard-of-hearing children. All have one common denominator: they are functioning on a retarded learning level. Many of them have been diagnosed as institutional cases. Their parents have been told they were hopeless. Their teachers have been told they were hopeless. This diagnosis we would not accept. By opening our hearts and minds to these children, we have helped them to do amazing things, things that no one thought were possible. The teacher does not set a limit to what these children can do; they set the limits themselves. From time to time they may stay on a plateau; then they begin to grow again.

We provide a reading readiness program from the first day these children enter school, and create a classroom atmosphere in which they can begin to read when they are ready. One child may be ready soon; another child, a year later. Consequently, we have different levels of reading going on in the one classroom. The children work individually and in three reading groups: beginners, second year readers, and an advanced group. In this language arts program the emphasis is on communication through speaking, writing, and reading.

Specific Objectives and Illustrations of Procedures Used

Group 1, Beginners:

1. To introduce new words on the chalkboard.
2. To give kinesthetic practice for words that cause special difficulty.
3. To provide varied practice on words, phrases, sentences, and stories.
4. To encourage use of words in original sentences.
5. To check on pupils' comprehension of new words and sentences.

T. Boys and girls, do you know what this is? (Pointing to microphone used in the demonstration).

P. A microphone.

T. What does a microphone do? How does it help us? How does it work?

P. When you talk into it, the ladies and gentlemen can hear you.

T. Yes, it makes what we say louder. Would you like to introduce yourselves now?

P. My name is David (Others in the group give their names).

T. Some of the boys and girls aren't here today. Can you help me remember who isn't here? We'll call these the absent boys and girls (writes it on the board). David, who is not here today?

P. Sharon? (T. writes names on board as pupils give them).

T. Yes, that's right.

P. Isabel.

T. Isabel. That's right. What kind of a dance does Isabel like to do?

P. Spanish.

T. Who else does Spanish dances?

P. Ann.

T. Who is the boy we help talk a little louder?

P. Jimmy.

T. Jimmy, that's right. And who is the girl who likes to dance all the time?

P. Joyce.

T. Joyce. That's right. Joyce has been sick. Let's read these names. Whose name is this? (Points to name of Jenny.)

P. Jenny. (T. continues with reading of names. Pupils have difficulty with *David* and *Danny*, *Jimmy* and *Jenny*. They need practice and instruction in middle and final sounds.)

T. Let's go to the blackboard and write our own names. (Pupils write and then read their names.) T. writes on the blackboard, "David is a girl" then asks, "What's wrong with this sentence?"

P. David is a ———.

T. Lucy, tell me what this word is.

P. Girl.

T. David is a ———.

P. Girl.

T. Is that right? What word should be there?

P. Boy.

T. Who can write *boy* in this sentence?
(P writes "boy" on board to correct sentence.)

T. Very good. Now the sentence is right. (T. also writes directions which pupils carry out, *e.g.*, "Sara, come here.")

Group 2, Second-year Readers:

1. To read silently new material.
2. To apply phonetic analysis to new words.
3. To develop and use a word list related to the social studies project.
4. To check understanding of all vocabulary words and to dramatize words difficult to explain.
5. To help pupils acquire a background of information so that they can converse intelligently with anyone whom they meet.

T. Sara, I'm going to let you read a story. Would you like a story about pioneers, or about bears and tigers?
P. About bears and tigers.
T. As you read, see if you can find something funny in the story. Read it silently first and then you can read it out loud.
T. (to other pupils) Here are your workbooks with exercises for you to do as usual.
P. (reads aloud to another small group,) "Tony and Bob and Smoky at the Parade." ("Smoky" is incorrectly read for "Spooky.")
T. Look at this word carefully (points to *Spooky*).
P. Spooky (reads sentence with *Spooky* instead of *Smoky*).
T. Good. (The other boys read this sentence with him.) What is the story about?
P. About Tony and the wagon (look at picture of the wagon).
T. What words describe the wagon?
P's (mention *wheels*, *little*, *box;* they pronounce and spell the new words.)
T. Any other words?
P. Tony's.
T. How do you spell *Tony's?* What kind of a *T* does it have?
P. Capital.

T. Why?
P. It's the name of a boy.
T. That's right. Names of people always begin with capitals. Let's see if you can make up a story of your own about that little wagon.
P. Can we use any other words?
T. Yes, any words you want to.
P's (Write and read their stories.)
T. (Discusses with Sara the story she read silently.) Did you find any words you didn't know?
P. (points to word *devour*.)
T. Let's look it up in the dictionary. What does it mean?
P. To swallow or eat up.
T. When the Tiger said, "Oh, no, he would devour you," what was he worried about?
P. That he would be eaten up.
T. Right. If you devour something, do you eat it slowly or quickly?
P. Quickly.
T. Would you gobble or sip?
P. Gobble.
T. Joyce, what does *devour* mean?
P. To eat it up, eat something all up quickly.
T. (begins discussion of social studies project)
What does the word *transportation* mean?
P. To move away from some place.
T. Yes, Tony was using a way of transportation, wasn't he? What was it?
P. A wagon.
T. Help me spell it (writes it on the board). Let's see how quickly you can list all the ways of transportation.
P's (Mention boat, train, airplane, car, truck, bicycle, tricycle, taxi. They spell each word as teacher writes it on board. They use the tracing method (Fernald) for words which give them special difficulty. They review these words by finding them on the board.)

T. Let's see how quickly you can give me the definition of some words. What is a definition?
P. The meaning of a word.
T. Right. What does *explore* mean?
P. To find.
T. Give a sentence using it.
P. To find a new country.
P. The pioneers followed the explorers.
T. The explorers were first and then the pioneers came. Who were the pioneers?
P. Frontiersmen?
T. Right. What did these frontiersmen do?
P. They had to walk on foot and find grass for the sheep.
T. What were they looking for?
P. Good land for crops.
T. If they wanted to grow crops, what did they have to take with them?
P. Hoe and their property.
T. Their hoe and all their property. And what else?
P. Seeds.

Group 3, the Advanced Group: Three pupils worked as a team; one read orally, one checked for mistakes, and one asked comprehensive questions. They used tape recordings to show improvement in oral reading and discussion. The pupils' previous experiences, pictures, films, and books are used to develop meanings. Art, music, crafts, and dramatics are correlated with reading.

All groups need worthwhile, interesting activities; specific, clear directions and questions; varied repetition to insure learning; praise for every move in the right direction; records of individual pupil progress in every reading skill.

It will also be noted that, in the beginners' group, vocabulary was personalized; it was taught in connection with the pupils' names and activities of immediate interest and use to them. The teacher gave these pupils a choice whenever possible as, for example, the choice of stories. He also helped the pupils define their purpose in reading the story. He encouraged thinking and word study in many ways; for example, in finding words that described the wagon, in speculating about the frontiersmen and their needs, and in drawing on the pupils' experience to enrich the meaning of words. New words and sentences were first spoken, then the pupil wrote them, then immediately read them – a sound linguistic sequence.

Questions and Comments

What changes have taken place in individual children who have been in the program several years? One fourteen-year-old girl has been in the program five years. Her original test score was from fifty to sixty I.Q. She is now testing around seventy I.Q., an increase of about twenty-five points. She can read books suitable for other adolescents of her age, and can give an accurate account of the political activities she faithfully reads about in the newspaper.

Another girl, who has been in the special class for four years, had encephalitis at fifteen months and was diagnosed as having "gross brain damage." Her parents were advised to put her in a custodial situation. She is one of our most reliable messengers and has adapted well to the school in other ways. In the beginning she spoke only one or two words at a time. Now she speaks in complete sentences and, at times in paragraphs. She still has some speech problems which affect her reading and spelling.

How long is the reading period? Although it is generally said that the attention span of mentally retarded children is short, we spend forty minutes on these varied reading activities. If the activities – the reading material itself and the social relations involved – are interesting to these children, they will keep working during the entire period.

How do you use TV in your program? These children all view TV and are authorities on TV programs. For example, "Wagon Train" is a real situation to them. We have discussed it in class: why the pioneers had wagon trains, why wagon trains came before railroads, why railroads could not be built until steel was invented. When I reviewed our social studies work on pioneers and settlers, I was amazed at the wealth of knowledge they had gained through being given information and being encouraged to use it. In our discussions they have gained confidence in their ability to express their ideas. They have also lost their fear of using new words.

On what basis are these pupils placed in a special class? Usually they have been examined by medical doctors, by the crippled children's clinic, by the guidance clinic, and by school psychologists. Very important also is the teacher's comprehensive report on the pupil's behavior in a regular classroom. There are test scores on all the pupils sent to the special class. We do some retesting as the need is indicated.

One of the boys reversed letters in writing his name. Do reversals occur in his other writing? Most of the pupils show reversal tendencies. We try to correct them but not make an issue of this tendency unless it is wrecking their progress. It often takes months to correct reversals. When the reversal of letters is restricted to a few words only, the tendency may have got started when the child was beginning to print these words.

When these pupils become too old for elementary school, are similar opportunities for them provided in junior high school? Each year about 10 per cent of the enrollment in the special education department return to regular classrooms. We cooperate with both elementary and junior high schools in providing a modified program in which they take reading and shop and other courses of a practical nature.

What are the home backgrounds of these children? There is almost as wide a variety as you would find in any elementary class.

Do you have a parent group? Yes, we have a very active parent organization. It is essential that parents understand the handicaps and the abilities of their children.

Chapter Five

The foregoing chapters have replenished the teacher's reservoir of ideas for identifying, understanding, and working with four major types of reading problem. From this reservoir he can select the ideas appropriate to his pupils and appealing to him.

Summary and Concluding Remarks

AMELIA MELNIK

Methods and Procedures

There are many emphases which have emerged from this conference which should guide our further work in improving the reading of all children. One I should like to highlight is the need for putting the process of reading into the broad context of the child's experience. More and more our selection of material and instruction should stem from this basis. Traditionally we have focussed on the use of published material for reading instruction. We need to tap another equally important and perhaps more useful source of material; that is the material which appears in the course of everyday life experiences for which the learner has immediate use and application. Certainly experiences stories fall in this category. Moreover, there is a wealth of instructional material that pupils themselves contribute daily in the course of their classroom work. More and more we should use the best examples of pupils' written work as a basis for instruction in reading improvement. Children need and welcome opportunities to learn from one another as well as from the textbook and workbook.

Of utmost importance, regardless of the source of instructional material, is the absolute need for the teacher to analyze first the material itself in terms of (1) what she hopes the pupils will gain from their reading, and (2) the process by which they might achieve these desired outcomes. Such an analysis will clarify for the teacher the kind of reading instruction appropriate for a given selection and suggest procedures to guide children's learning. In this way the need to vary rate and method of reading according to the purpose of the reader and the material to be read becomes apparent to both the teacher and the pupils.

Moreover, since learning continues long after formal education has been terminated, pupils ought to become more aware of the methods by which they are learning while instruction is being given. Since reading is a tool of learning, it may be that their understanding of the reading process and how they learn is more important than the content which is used to develop their reading ability. Such knowledge enables pupils to continue independently in a program of reading improvement.

A final goal toward which we must strive is that of being more thorough in our teaching of reading. Too often our instruction is limited to a simple process of teach-test. If learning of essential processes and concepts is to be complete, then our teaching process must be extended to include, first, appraisal to guide instruction, followed by plenty of practice before testing to gain evidence of learning. Thus, the teaching-learning process should follow the pattern of appraisal-instruction-practice-testing.

In striving to achieve these important goals, we shall meet many baffling problems on the way. To keep us on our path I should like to quote a rhyme from Mother Goose which Dr. Strang introduced to me first many years ago:

> For every evil under the sun
> There is a remedy or there be none.
> If there be one, go and find it –
> If there be none, never mind it.

RUTH STRANG

The Role of the Teacher

A wide range of procedures has been suggested for identifying, understanding, and helping retarded readers. At one extreme is the teacher's unrecorded observation on which he acts as need is indicated. At the other extreme is the study of individual intelligence and achievement tests, developmental and school histories, records of interviews, and other specialized techniques and resources. The most difficult part of any comprehensive diagnostic procedure is to interpret the information that has been obtained, to see how each item reinforces or contradicts the hypotheses one has formed thus far, and in the end to perceive how this all combines to indicate what kind of help the child needs to improve his reading.

The role of the teacher in this process is clearly recognized. Teachers are people of importance. Their techniques serve as a screening device for differentiating the causes of reading retardation. The information they give to the psychologist is of vital importance in helping him make his diagnosis. Teachers can often give immediate help as soon as they recognize the difficulty; they can bridge the gap between theoretical knowledge and practical assistance. A background of understanding sharpens the teacher's awareness of the needs of individual pupils; some can be helped with a comment, a smile, a recommendation for recreational reading or practice material, a word of approval, or a suggestion as to how they can cope with a difficult situation.

Teachers are important members of a team that includes parents, reading teachers and consultants, special school personnel, and available community consultants. The team approach enables us to look at the reading problems as one aspect of the total person in the total social situation. Since home-school relations are so important, teachers should have training in interview techniques so that they can communicate more effectively with both children and parents.

Our main focus should be on developmental reading and the prevention of reading difficulties, rather than on remedial work per se. In a sense, remedial work with retarded readers, which is so necessary at present, is developmental; we start where the individual is and continue his reading development from that point as fast and as far as he can go. But reading development begins at birth. The preschool years are a prelude to reading instruction in the primary grades. On all levels, teachers handle reading problems as they arise; they keep in mind a sequential development of reading attitudes, interests, and skills from kindergarten to college.

In working with mentally retarded children, we should teach them what they can learn and what they can use. We should not take a fatalistic attitude toward these children, but help each one to realize his full ability. And we should try to forestall the secondary emotional problems that may arise from feelings of frustration and inferiority.

There are individual differences among the children in each of the groups described: the mentally retarded, the bilingual, the emotionally disturbed, and the able retarded readers. Motivation plays a dominant part in all our work with retarded readers. Many are depressed by previous experiences of failure and frustration. They think of themselves as persons who cannot learn to read. They may even have become so accustomed to their reading handicap that they resist changing. When a little boy was told he could do anything if he wanted to, he asked, "But how do you get to want to?"

There are many immediate motivations. Even brain-damaged children respond to specific incentives. For example, one child who had apparently forgotten all the words she had learned the day before was able to recognize all of them correctly when she was stimulated by playing the role of teacher and correcting the mistakes that her reading teacher purposely made. Older boys who were seriously retarded in reading have been motivated to acquire the reading skills they were capable of learning when they faced the need to pass the examination for a driver's license, to fill out applications for a job, or to read the letters written by their girl friends.

We should not make teachers feel guilty by setting an impossibly high level of aspiration. There are some pupils who cannot profit by the best reading instruction in the world, because of certain hereditary and uncorrected environmental conditions. The fact that we have many unanswered question should be a challenge, not a cause for discouragement. Our attitude toward retarded readers should not be that of the pessimist who sees a calamity in every opportunity, but that of the optimist who sees an opportunity in every calamity.

APPENDIX A

Introduction to the Conference

Hollis Moore, Jr.

As dean of the College of Education, I have been asked to give to the Reading Conference a "mere welcome," but this is not a mere conference. It is not only one which we have anticipated with real pleasure, but it is also one which is striking out in a bold new direction for conferences. The speeches tonight are taped, and by this method we are able to bring you four outstanding speakers.

Let me not only welcome you to this conference and wish for you the kind of intellectual stimulation which we expect from such an enterprise, but also let me share with you a quotation which will illustrate the importance of reading here, today, and tomorrow.

"It ought to be a leading object in our schools to teach the art of reading. It ought to occupy threefold more time than it does. We had rather have a child return to us from a school a first-rate reader than a first-rate performer on the piano. Let the same pains be devoted to reading as are required to form an accomplished performer on an instrument. The art of reading requires a constant exercise, but it also demands continual and close reflection in thought and the finest discrimination of ideas."

I'm sure you will agree with this charge that the teaching of reading is today tremendously important. However, I must admit that the quotation just read is from the preface to *The National Preceptor* by Jay Olney, published at Hartford in 1833.

I have dug further into my collection of old textbooks and have found in Sanders' *The School Reader*, published in 1841, a list of rules for reading. And rule number one is, "You should learn the definition of every word which you do not already understand. It is impossible to read a sentence well unless you understand its meaning."

And from McGuffey's *Eclectic Fourth Reader*, the 1853 edition, "The great object to be accomplished in reading is to convey to the hearer the ideas and feelings of the writer. In order to do this it is necessary that the reader should himself thoroughly *understand* those sentiments and feelings. It is true he may pronounce the words as traced upon the page, but ideas received in this manner bear the same resemblance to the reality that the dead body does to the living spirit. No scholar should be permitted to read anything which he does not easily understand."

I hope this brief plunge back into two or three musty old books will help give us an historical perspective for this conference on reading—reading for understanding, reading for communication of ideas, reading for full and complete intellectual growth.

APPENDIX B

Selected Bibliography

CHAPTER ONE

THE ABLE RETARDED READER

Bland, Phyllis. "Helping Bright Students who Read Poorly," *The Reading Teacher*, 9:209-214 (April 1956).

Fernald, Grace. *Remedial Techniques in Basic School Subjects*. New York: McGraw-Hill Book Company, 1943.

Mooney, John (editor). *Reading Disability: Progress and Research Needs in Dyslexia*. Baltimore: Johns Hopkins Press, 1962.

Pollack, Myron Frank W. *Reading Problems and Problem Readers*. (Reading Case Studies). New York: David McKay Company, 1963.

Robinson, H. Alan (editor). *The Under-Achiever in Reading*. Conference on Reading, University of Chicago. Chicago: Chicago University Press, 1962.

Robinson, Helen (editor). The following Supplementary Educational Monographs are published by the University of Chicago Press:

Corrective Reading in the Classroom and Clinic. No. 79, 1953.

Promoting Maximal Reading Growth among Able Readers. No. 81, 1954.

Materials for Reading. No. 86, 1957.

Reading Instruction in Various Patterns of Grouping. No. 89, 1959.

Evaluation of Reading. No. 88, 1958.

Controversial Issues and Promising Solutions in Reading. No. 91, 1961.

Robinson, Helen, *Why Pupils Fail in Reading.* Chicago: University of Chicago Press, 1946.

Roswell, Florence and Natchez, Gladys. *Reading Disability: Diagnosis and Treatment.* New York: Basic Books, 1964.

Strang, Ruth. *Diagnostic Teaching of Reading.* New York: McGraw-Hill Book Company, 1964.

Helping Your Child Improve His Reading. New York: E. P. Dutton, 1962.

Strang, Ruth et al. *The Improvement of Reading.* Third edition, New York: McGraw-Hill Company, 1961.

Teen-age Tales. Books 1-6 are on the 5th-6th grade level of reading difficulty; Books A, B, and C are on the 3rd-4th grade level of reading difficulty. Boston: D. C. Heath and Company, 1958-1962.

Chapter Two

Emotionally Disturbed Children

Bower, Eli M. *Early Identification of Emotionally Handicapped Children in School.* Springfield, Illinois: C. C. Thomas, 1960.

Ephron, Beulah K. *Emotional Difficulties in Reading.* New York: Julian Press, Inc., 1953.

Haring, Norris Grover. *Educating Emotionally Disturbed Children.* New York: McGraw-Hill Book Company, 1962.

Holmes, Jack A. "Emotional Factors and Reading Disability," *Reading Teacher,* 9:11-17 (October 1955).

Krippner, Stanley. "Sociopathic Tendencies and Reading Retardation in Children," *Exceptional Children,* 29:258-266 (February 1963).

Nardelli, Robert R. "Creative Reading Includes Emotional Factors," *Reading Teacher,* 9:5-10 (October 1955).

Riese, Hertha. *Heal the Hurt Child;* an approach through educational therapy with special reference to the extremely deprived Negro child. Chicago: University of Chicago Press, 1962.

Talmadge, Max and others. "Study of Experimental Methods for Teaching Emotionally Disturbed, Brain-damaged, Retarded Readers," *Journal of Educational Research*, 56:311-316 (February 1963). (Copies of detailed procedures and plans are available upon request from the authors: Emma Pendleton Bradley Hospital, Riverside, R.I.)

Witty, Paul A. "Reading Success and Emotional Adjustment," *Elementary English*, 27:281-296 (May 1950).

Young, Nancy and Galer, E. L. "Implications in Emotionally Caused Reading Retardation," *Elementary English*, 28:271-275 (May 1951).

CHAPTER THREE

"BILINGUAL" CHILDREN

Arizona State Department of Public Instruction. *Bibliography for Teachers of English as a Second Language*. Phoenix: Arizona State Department of Public Instruction, 1960.

Ashton-Warner, Sylvia. *Teacher*. New York: Simon and Schuster, 1963.

Bumpass, Faye L. *Teaching Young Students English as a Foreign Language*. New York: American Book Company, 1963.

Condie, Le Roy. "Teaching English as a Second Language in Kindergarten in New Mexico," an unpublished dissertation. University of New Mexico, 1961.

English for Today. A six-volume series accompanied by tapes and records. New York: McGraw-Hill Book Company, 1962-1964.

Finochehiaro, Mary. *English as a Second Language: From Theory to Practice*. New York: Regents Publishing Company, 1964.

Fries, Charles C. *Linguistics and Reading*. New York: Holt, Rinehart and Winston, 1963.

(consultant). *American English Series for the Study of English as a Second Language*. Books 1-2, Pauline M. Rojas and Staff. Books 3-6, Adrian L. Hull and others. Boston: D. C. Heath and Company, 1957. See also *Teachers' Guides*.

Kitchin, A. T. and Allen, V. F. *Reader's Digest Readings in English as a Second Language*. Several volumes, Pleasantville, N.Y.: Reader's Digest, 1953-1964.

Lado, Robert. *Language Teaching—A Scientific Approach.* New York: McGraw-Hill, 1964.

Lefevre, Carl A. *Linguistics and the Teaching of Reading.* New York: McGraw-Hill Book Company, 1964.

Newsletter. Published monthly from September-June by the Division of Indian Education of the New Mexico State Department of Education, Santa Fe.

Preschool Instructional Program for Non-English Speaking Children. Dallas, Texas: Texas Education Agency, February 1961.

Spanish-American Song and Game Book. New York: A. S. Barnes and Company, 1942.

Strang, Ruth. "Linguistically Handicapped: Learning English as a Second Language, a Theoretical Model," *Exceptional Children,* 30:14-16 (September 1963).

Tireman, Lloyd. *Teaching Spanish-speaking Children.* Albuquerque, New Mexico: University of New Mexico, 1948.

U. S. Department of Health, Education and Welfare. *Improving English Skills of Culturally Different Youth.* Washington, D.C.: U. S. Government Printing Office, 1964.

Wall, Leon. *Problems in Teaching English to Navajo Children.* Ann Arbor, Michigan: University Microfilms, 1963.

Ware, Kay. "English Programs for the Culturally Different: Significant Aspects of the St. Louis Program," *Elementary English,* 40:611-614 (October 1963).

Zintz, Miles. *Education Across Cultures.* Dubuque, Iowa: W. C. Brown Book Company, 1963.

"Indian Children are Different," *The New Mexico School Review,* 40:26-27 (October 1960).

Zintz, Miles and Tireman, Lloyd. "Factors Influencing Learning a Second Language," *Education,* 81:310-313 (January 1961).

Zintz, Miles and Yandell, Maurine. "Some Difficulties which Indian Children Encounter with Idioms in Reading," *The Reading Teacher,* 14:256-259 (March 1961).

Chapter Four

The Mentally Retarded

Cruickshank, William M. *A Teaching Method for Brain-injured and Hyperactive Children.* Syracuse, New York: Syracuse University Press, 1961.

Davy, Ruth A. "Adaptation of Progressive-choice Method for Teaching Reading to Retarded Children, *American Journal of Mental Deficiency*, 67:274-280 (September 1962).

Gallagher, James J. *The Tutoring of Brain-injured Mentally Retarded Children.* Springfield, Illinois: C. C. Thomas, 1960.

Holbrook, David. *English for the Rejected:* Training literacy in the lower streams of the secondary school. New York: Cambridge University Press, 1964.

Johnson, George O. *Education for the Slow Learners.* New York: Prentice Hall, 1963.

Kephart, Newell C. *The Slow Learner in the Classroom.* Columbus, Ohio: Charles E. Merrill Books, 1960.

Kirk, Samuel A. *Teaching Reading to Slow Learning Children.* Boston: Houghton-Mifflin Company, 1950.

Educating Exceptional Children. Boston: Houghton-Mifflin Company, 1962.

"Reading Problems of Slow Learners," Chicago: Conference on Reading, University of Chicago, 1962.

and Bateman, B. "Diagnosis and Remediation of Learning Disabilities," *Exceptional Children*, 29:73-78 (October 1962).

"The Slow Learner," *Education*, 81 (February 1962). The entire issue is devoted to this topic.

Chapter Five

Summary and Concluding Remarks

Stahlecker, Lotar V. "Motivating the Slow Learner to Read," *The High School Journal*, 46:78-82 (December 1962).

Tansley, A. E. *The Education of Slow Learning Children.* London: Routledge and I. Paul, 1960.